# FIVE STAR PRAISE for *MENTAL TOUGHNESS FOR WOMEN LEADERS*

When a former undercover and counterintelligence agent for the FBI retires in glory and dives into researching what makes some women resilient, resonant and grounded leaders of women and men – then decides to share what she's learned, it makes for captivating reading. What I most admire is her candor, actionable insights based on her own experiences and her conversational yet concise writing style. This was an engrossing read. Quy shows how any of us can develop the mental toughness needed to succeed at work and in life. Rather than shrinking back into "ought to" or "not go enough" or "always put others first" admonitions many of us women hear and absorb, Quy describes how living fully, using our best talents and following our true path is actually healthier for those around us too.

—Kare Anderson, author of *Mutuality Matters, Moving From Me to We, Walk Your Talk, Resolving Conflict Sooner,* and *Getting What You Want*

This is a must-read from the leadership expert, LaRae Quy. While the book is tailored to women, these leadership lessons know no gender boundaries. Ms. Quy brings a blend of her experience, wisdom and practicality to create a roadmap for leadership success. This book helps you access your own inner strength to be the best you can be.

—Susanne Lyons, former VP Marketing, Visa

I had the joy of reading LaRae Quy's book recently, Mental Toughness for Women Leaders. She brings a wonderful blend of life experience and wisdom to her writing. Being a woman in a leadership position, I am always looking for ways to improve my leadership style

and attack difficult situations with grace. This book has given me clear insight how to improve on techniques I already use. I would highly recommend this book to women or men in any type of leadership role.
—Douglas Glover, attorney

This book isn't just a list of 52 tips and tricks, it's based on real-word experience with proven techniques to boost your mental toughness. It puts you in the driver's seat to get in control of your emotions, call on your courage and create success. This book is filled with stories and strategies that you can put to use immediately. A must read for men and women that want to cultivate their mental toughness.
—Allison Polin, Break the Frame Consulting

This book brings an honest been-there-done-that spirit to the conversation on women's leadership. It is possible to embrace our best female attributes and at the same time be a strong inspiration for others. Female and Strength are not contradictory terms. LaRae Quy shares a practical, easy-to-follow roadmap for making it so.
—Karin Hurt, author of *Overcoming An Imperfect Boss*

This is an outstanding book that everyone needs to read. Put it at the top of your list and learn how to be a warrior in life and in business. Every once in a while you read a book that wakes you up and ignites change. This one will do just that for you.
—Tammy Kling, co-author of *The Compass, Exit Row, Live!, The Transparent Leader, There's More To Life Than the Corner Office,* and *Searching For My Piece of the Soul*

LaRae Quy's latest book is jammed packed with great information and insights. The action plans and tips are set up so that you can set the book down and start to implement them immediately into your own life. The great thing about reading LaRae's books is that her style of writing makes me feel like she and I are sitting down together at the kitchen table and coming up with a plan on how to implement these things in my life. I also love the fact that she cuts through all of the gloss, build up, and fluff that is usually in a lot of the books on the market today. This is a great leadership book, whether you are male or female!

—Chris Schenk, healthcare consultant

In her new book, "Mental Toughness For Women Leaders", LaRae Quy delivers a treasure trove of insights, information and practical tools to catalyze leadership. Through her unique perspective and captivating storytelling as an ex-FBI agent, Quy offers powerful and realistic ways to overcome rough patches in our lives and bounce back with dignity and triumph. A book not to miss if you are ready to grow mental toughness.

—Terri Klass, Terri Klass Consulting

Developing mental strength is valuable no matter your gender and LaRae delivers keen insights and practical ways to be mindful, present, and thoughtfully engaging in our everyday leadership. The structure of the book is excellent, highlighting a key principle and then delivering key tips on how to lead and live by these principles. In other words, LaRae offers steps to turn words and thoughts into actions... an essential practice for any growth-minded leaders. My advice is to read this book cover-to-cover to grasp the ideas and practices to gain mental strength and then start each week with one of the tips, putting it into full practice and learning from what is experienced. What will happen through the time is you will become a more self-aware leader who is engaging others to take performance to new levels of achievement. Now that is strength!

—Jon Mertz, Founder, Thin Difference

# Mental Toughness for Women Leaders

Also By LaRae Quy

# Secrets of a Strong Mind

What My Years As An FBI
Counterintelligence Agent Taught
Me About Leadership And
Empowerment—And How To
Make It Work For You

Author's website
www.LaRaeQuy.com

# Mental Toughness for Women Leaders

## 52 Tips to Recognize and Utilize Your Greatest Strengths

LaRae Quy

MTC

THE MENTAL TOUGHNESS CENTER

San Francisco

*Mental Toughness for Women Leaders: 52 Tips To Recognize And Utilize Your Greatest Strengths* is a work of non-fiction. Some names and identifying data have been changed.

Published by the Mental Toughness Center

ISBN 978-1502420961

Printed in the United States of America

*FIRST EDITION*

Book design by Anne Doyle @ a design

*For Roger*

*Strength doesn't come from what you can do. It comes from overcoming the things you once thought you couldn't do. Mental toughness is believing you can prevail in your circumstances rather than believing your circumstances will change*—LaRae Quy

# TABLE OF CONTENTS

# INTRODUCTION

When I entered the FBI Academy as a new agent, I was surrounded by other classmates who were mostly men, athletes, and either former military or law enforcement officers. Each of us would be spending the next four months training alongside one another in defensive tactics, firearms, and federal law.

When our instructors used the phrase mental toughness, it conjured up images of great masses of muscle bulldozing their way through obstacles and roadblocks to reach their goal. For me, mental toughness was the sheer willpower of refusing to slow down until the end goal was reached. Movies and popular novels depict mentally tough FBI agents as walking with a swagger and bouncing bodies from walls as they beat the opposition into submission.

Much of the FBI Academy centered around physical fitness, and in my early days, mental toughness was equated with how well a trainee boxed, how many pushups they could pump out, and how fast they could run.

Did I mention that I was a fashion buyer in a fancy department store before I was recruited as an FBI Agent? You can imagine how well that was received by guys who chewed glass and spit nails for recreation. The physical fitness tests were very difficult for me because I never have been an athlete. There were many times I thought I would never make it through the rigors of the FBI Academy, and there were many of my fellow agents who thought I did not belong there, either.

I remember the kindness of a few instructors who encouraged me, but their job was to sift out those who did not have the mental toughness to make it as an FBI Agent. Did I have it? To answer that question, I needed to think a little deeper about what makes a strong mind, a mind that could bend but not break.

Many of my instructors waited for me to quit. When I wouldn't, they set their dry little hearts into uncovering the stuff from which I was made—the intimidation was not only physical, it was mental as well. During the defensive tactics tests, my performance was reviewed by a committee of coaches, not just an assistant coach like everyone else. I was placed under intense scrutiny and if my elbow did not bend down far enough for each and every pushup, that pushup was not counted.

Performing in a gym is like being in a glass cage; everyone can see the results. And your performance is there for every critic to observe and pass judgment on. Whether it's fair or not is not the issue—when your profile is raised, everyone is watching.

Did I think I was being singled out? Not really, because the truth of the matter was this: either I had what it took to get through the Academy or I didn't. I didn't expect to get special treatment because I was a minority—in my graduation class of forty agents, eight of them were women. I did muster the points to get through the defensive tactics portion of the FBI Academy. I will be the first to tell you that I only had the minimum score to graduate, while many of my classmates set records in the long distance run and pushups.

What never got publicized was that I did incredibly well in the written tests and firearms. Those were personal victories, but I clung to them when times got tough.

It wasn't until after I had graduated from the Academy and spent several years as a counterintelligence and undercover agent that I realized the true definition of mental toughness: it is believing I would prevail in my circumstances rather than believing my circumstances would change.

Leadership is not about blaming others, whining about your situation, or refusing to take responsibility. It is about finding ways to develop a strong mind so you bounce back when hit by a rough patch in life. There are two steps to developing a strong mind:

Step 1. Excavate the significance of your own stories and experiences

Step 2. Grow your brain

We all have incredible stories if we will give ourselves both permission to mine their significance and the time to understand their impact on the way we think. It's hard work, and for many, our past brings up unpleasant memories. Pretending those memories don't exist, or suppressing them, does not help us as we make our way through life. Instead, learn what these memories have to teach us—and very importantly, move on.

Research and science is showing us ways we can re-wire the way we think, because mental toughness is all about growing the brain. You want a stronger mind? Build a stronger brain.

That is what this book is about.

What follows is a collection of experiences and research-based tactics on how to build a strong mind taken from the scientists who discovered them. While many of the experiences I share with you are my own, you also have stories that need to be uncovered and examined—they have a lot to teach you. Take ownership of your own life; you may not have had much control over where you came from, but you are in complete control over where you're going.

The advice and tactics in this book have been field-tested, and best of all, they are concise and practical.

We are all busy and need to make the most of our time and energy. This is not so much of a "how-to" book as it is an "I-can" book. There is nothing more powerful than the human brain once we have the tools that give us the mental toughness we need to succeed in life and business.

## HOW TO USE THIS BOOK

It's important to start off with a basic understanding of mental toughness.

1. Mental toughness is not something you are born with; it is something you can learn.
2. Mental toughness is training the mind to always be on your side, not sometimes helping you or sometimes working against you.

I am an investigator by training, so one of the very first things I learned is that while theories are nice, evidence is better. So I'm going to ask you to treat this book like an investigation—a data-based approach to learning how to uncover the secrets of mental toughness. You need to make yourself the subject of your own real-world investigation. I'm going to be presenting investigative steps on how you can change your thinking about the obstacles and barriers you face in life. After I've laid out these steps, I'm going to ask you to gather evidence about your own thinking and then hold that data up for close scrutiny to see what is true for you and what works for you.

This book is built around the idea that you are responsible for developing your own strong mind. You have the capabilities; all you are lacking are the tools. This book will give them to you. Keep your mental toolbox handy, and use this book as a reference when you hit a bump on the road or find that life has taken an unexpected turn.

The book is divided into four categories, each of which are essential components of mental toughness to help you overcome obstacles and break through barriers:

1) Use Emotional Intelligence: Develop the self-awareness to predict, and control, your response to adversity and obstacles. Awareness of others is also essential if you want to lead effectively.

2) Bullet-Proof The Brain: Upgrade the way your brain works by re-wiring it. There are

several simple, yet effective science-based ways to develop the brain of a leader.

3) Find Your Inner Warrior: Stay cool under pressure, grow stronger from turmoil in your life, and move forward when feeling overwhelmed. It's a matter of being brutally honest with yourself and choosing how you respond, rather than react, to life's obstacles.

4) Predict Your Success: Move toward peak performance by visualizing your success, juggling life and work, and discovering ways you can beat the odds. It requires a mindset that is focused on success and breaking through barriers.

Each section contains three chapters and a series of tips. The tips themselves are brief—but they are explained in detail so you will understand the thinking behind each one. If you're interested in the research behind them,

I've included a List of References in the back that explain the neuroscience that supports the tip.

# SECTION ONE

*How to use Emotional Intelligence*

We are frequently taught that mental toughness is about willpower, persistence, resilience, and determination—and that if we cannot train our mind to think in these terms, we cannot be mentally tough. While this statement is not entirely false, it is not entirely true, either—more precisely, it is incomplete.

There are many secrets to a strong mind. One of the most ignored is interpreting and managing our emotions and the emotions of others. The ability to be emotionally intelligent requires a set of skills that can be learned.

Self-awareness is essential if leaders expect to make good decisions when they respond to a crisis or unexpected events in life. Self-awareness illuminates ways we can use emotions to tap into our best selves and produce amazing results.

Great leaders understand that the ability to read people's needs and desires, whether they are expressed or not, allows them to respond to those needs. Human Resource specialist Meghan Biro sums it up in this quote:

*"The ability to reach people in a way that transcends the intellectual and rational is the mark of a great leader."*

I would add that a significant skill of a great leader is the ability to reach both ourselves and others in ways that are truly meaningful.

This first section is about creating awareness of your emotional literacy and channeling that awareness into your leadership style. The tips cover many ways you can increase your learning of how to handle yourself and others, because emotional intelligence is a strong predictor of who will become successful.

# Chapter 1

# *Mental Toughness Requires Emotional Intelligence*

I've been frequently asked how the "touchy-feely" aspect of emotional intelligence was viewed by the FBI agents with whom I worked alongside for 24 years. I would be the first to say that the FBI is not a touchy-feely sort of organization; on the other hand, emotional intelligence is an important tool for agents required to recruit human intelligence (humint) sources and interview suspects.

Many believe that mental toughness is a leader's ability to plow through emotions and feelings without being touched by them so they can continue to march stalwartly onward. It's not that simple.

Leaders with mental toughness need to identify and control emotions, not only of themselves but of others as well. Mental toughness is not ignoring feelings or refusing to express them; instead, it is the intelligence to perceive, use, understand, and manage our emotions.

Awareness and curiosity about their own emotions, as well as those of others, places leaders in a stronger position to not only recognize the negative ones but to anticipate how they could spin out of control.

Emotional Intelligence has four parts: self-awareness, managing our emotions, empathy, and social skills. Whether men or women have an edge in emotional intelligence matters more than ever in the workplace as more companies are beginning to recognize the role of emotional intelligence in successful leaders.

According to Daniel Goleman, women tend to be better at emotional empathy than men. This is the sort of empathy that encourages rapport and chemistry. When women are sympathizing with someone, their brain mimics what the person feels. Many have speculated that women are better at mimicry and recognizing body language because they've spent more time with infants and small children.

If the other person is upset, women's brains tend to stay with those feelings; but men's brains tend to try and solve the problem that's creating the disturbance.

While it's tempting to judge one response as better or more effective than the other, researchers determined that when looking at top leadership performers, gender differences in emotional intelligence abilities wash out: The men are as good as the women, the women as good as the men, across the board.

## THE ONE SKILL EVERY GREAT LEADER POSSESSES

FBI agents who work undercover are given a series of psychological tests to determine their level of self-awareness. Without self-awareness, agents would not be able to predict their responses when confronted with the unknown that accompanies undercover work.

Psychological tests are constructed and administered by the FBI's Behavioral Science Unit. I spent a week being assessed by FBI instructors and attending classes intended to drill into me the importance of emotional intelligence if I was to become a successful undercover agent.

Since self-awareness is the ability to accurately perceive your own emotions, your competence as a leader rests on your ability to stay alert to them so you can manage your behavior in different situations.

A high degree of self-awareness requires a willingness to tolerate the discomfort of focusing on feelings that may be negative. It can take a strong mind to move through that discomfort, but it's essential because the more you know about yourself, the better you can predict your reactions.

*"He who knows others is wise. He who knows himself is enlightened"*—Lao Tzu

It's important to understand, however, that self-awareness is not about discovering the deep, dark secrets of your inner world. Instead, it is about developing a straightforward and honest understanding of what makes you tick.

Self-awareness is the one skill that every great leader possesses. If you are self-aware, you are far more likely to pursue the right opportunities, use your strengths, and keep your emotions from holding you back.

## UNDERSTANDING OUR EMOTIONS IS KEY TO CONTROLLING THEM

As an FBI agent, I was surrounded by law enforcement officers who had a strong sense of right and wrong. They were motivated by their moral emotions to move into adverse and dangerous situations because they believed in protecting the well-being of others.

Research from the University of Virginia has shown that emotions are strongly connected to our morality—the ability to tell right from wrong. For example, gratitude and indignation are both moral emotions; gratitude is a positive emotion that encourages reciprocal altruism, well-being, and appreciation. Indignation, on the other hand, is a negative emotion that is closely related to anger and revenge—it motivates individuals to punish cheaters.

Mental toughness strengthens our ability to distinguish positive emotions from negative ones. We can use this awareness to strengthen positive emotions like gratitude and control negative ones like anger.

Mental toughness is learning how to connect with those emotions that attract more of the things that represent our moral standards. In turn, we see ourselves as living and doing what is right.

We can all become more self-aware leaders if we learn how to read our own emotions.


## HOW CAN MENTALLY TOUGH WOMEN LEADERS USE EMOTIONAL INTELLIGENCE?


Leaders who label their own emotions, and those of others, do three things:

1) Identify what creates stress
2) Pinpoint what motivates positive behavior
3) Listen and talk in ways that resolve conflicts rather than escalate them

Self-discipline is not an attitude of harshness or limitations. Instead, it is an element of inner strength where you choose what you will make a priority. To become an expert, you will need to stick with it, practice, fail many times, find new approaches to attack the problem, and continue to study in your field until you find a path to success. This takes a discipline that will leave you with such deep skills that when confronted with obstacles and barriers, you will have the mental strength to do things faster, smarter, and better.

*"Mental toughness is many things and rather difficult to explain. It is combined with a perfectly disciplined will that refuses to give in. It's a state of mind—you could call it character in action"*—Vince Lombardi

Self-awareness is a critical skill for FBI agents who continually seek out ways to overcome obstacles and adversity. Self-awareness is being

# TIP #1 *Identify Your Emotional Hotspots*

One of the best ways to identify what creates unwanted stress is to learn what pushes emotional hotspots that create both positive and negative emotions. We all have buttons that produce predictable reactions. When specific ones are pushed, we can scream, throw tantrums, or burn with anger. Other buttons encourage us to express gratitude, thankfulness, and appreciation. Knowing who, or what, pushes our buttons and how it happens is critical to developing the ability to take control of the situation.

- Notice your emotions, thoughts, and behaviors as various situations unfold. *Note: This is a piece of advice that will be repeated throughout this book. Failing to notice your emotions when they show up uninvited and unexpected is one of the primary reasons you sabotage your own efforts to succeed.*

- Slow yourself down so the fast-thinking emotional part of your brain doesn't overtake the slower-thinking logical part of your brain. You often read how important it is to breathe slowly when you're stressed, and one of the benefits is that by taking deep breaths you automatically slow yourself down to where you can let your brains catch up with one another.

- Take the opportunity to pinpoint the specific circumstances that produce emotional reactions. This self-awareness will enable you to calibrate your reactions in the future. Identifying your emotional hotspots is vital if you plan to control your response so you can abolish unproductive behavior that sabotages your success.

# TIP #2 Dig Deep to Find Self-Awareness

Self-awareness begins by probing deeper to understand your entire range of emotions, including the negative ones. We know emotions often show up uninvited and unexpected; but instead of pretending negative ones don't exist, acknowledge them for what they are. Emotions serve an important purpose—they are clues to what you need to pay attention to in order to fully understand yourself.

Even when the emotions are painful, you need to:

- Pay attention to them.
- Trace them back to their origin to understand their purpose.
- Spend time looking for why this emotion surfaced at this time, who triggered it, and in what context?

Self-awareness provides you with the ability to understand why you do the things you do so you can choose your responses instead of reacting to situations around you. Successful people have a high level of self-awareness and are able to accurately assess information about their abilities, even when it is unflattering.

Once you know yourself and your limits, you know exactly what you're afraid of and exactly how hard to push against it.

If you are not willing to take a honest look at your abilities and identify where you need to improve, you will never move past your current circumstances. Those with self-knowledge do not worry when their radar comes up with something about themselves that is unflattering. The reason is because they are also acutely aware of their strengths.

To be successful, it is essential to have accurate information about your abilities so you can learn more efficiently and effectively.

# TIP #3

*Put Yourself Under Surveillance*

FBI agents routinely place the target of their investigation under surveillance to uncover patterns in their behavior. It is an essential first step in an FBI investigation. A surveillance log is kept, and once a target's normal routine is established, it's much easier to recognize aberrant behavior.

In the same way, you can put yourself under surveillance. Keep a log of everyday activities so you can pinpoint situations that influence your attitude or behavior. Rather than reviewing your daily activities as a linear recitation of facts and figures, scan them so you can identify highlights: specific experiences that produced a reaction or moved you in some way. Once those experiences have been identified, you can drill down further to see whether you responded the same way on other days or in different circumstances.

This will allow you move up your self-awareness level up a notch or two. Continue to learn more about yourself and what motivates you by asking, "What preoccupies my thinking?" "When am I most comfortable with myself?" "What do I notice first in others?" Personal surveillance can produce a mother-lode of important information about how you tick.

Picking apart and analyzing behavior becomes a mindset. Because of this, it is something that can be practiced by anyone at any time. For example, law enforcement officers often look at people around them in restaurants and airports and attempt to figure out their stories—such as what they do for a living, their mood, what they're thinking—based solely on observation.

This simple focused-awareness drill can train a person's mind to be clued in on what is going on with not only themselves, but the people around them as well.

# TIP #4

## *Cultivate Curiosity About Life*

Emotionally intelligent leaders can pinpoint what motivates positive behavior because they are curious. Curiosity is an important trait for geniuses, FBI agents working investigations, and anyone who wants to be emotionally intelligent. Curious people have active minds that are always asking questions and searching for answers, instead of passive minds.

People with a curious mindset are continually expecting and anticipating new information about events and situations. They are continually seeking information about how to perform at higher levels of competence.

Curious people seek new insight into the behavior of others, as well as themselves. They do not accept the world as it is without trying to dig deeper beneath the surface around them. This is why interviews and questioning are essential investigative steps for FBI agents. Using open-ended questions by starting them with these words—who, what, when, where, and how—are great ways to unlock information.

How many of us are truly curious about ourselves? Do we look at ourselves with an open and loving heart and mind, willing to understand whatever we might find? Or do we look at ourselves with a bunch of preconceived notions and shut our eyes to what we don't know?

Practicing curiosity about ourselves when we are not stressed helps us continue that process when we are stuck or confronted with obstacles. We can start by just looking at ourselves and being curious about what we find. The next step is to simply notice what we find without judging it as good or bad. Finally, we welcome what we find.

Developing the habit of being curious about ourselves makes it easier to predict our reactions when we're stressed or challenged in life. Once we understand our patterns of thinking and behaving, we possess the ability to choose our responses.

Curiosity is the foundation of life-long growth. If we remain curious, we remain teachable so that our minds and hearts grow larger with each passing day. We can retain our beginner's mind by always looking forward and discovering new experiences and uncovering new information.

Success seduces us into becoming set in our ways. "It's working," we say to ourselves, so we settle into comfort zones that begin to look more and more like ruts as we age. Curiosity is important for peak performance because it:

- Makes your mind active instead of passive
- Encourages you to be more observant of new ideas
- Opens up new worlds and possibilities
- Creates an adventurous response that leads you in a new direction

# TIP #5

## Develop Gratitude as a Power Emotion

Once you have identified what creates stress and pinpointed what motivates positive behavior, you will be able to tap into emotions that resolve conflicts rather than escalate them. One of the most powerful emotions for mentally tough leaders to develop is gratitude.

You can use mental toughness to strengthen your gratitude emotion and control the negative emotions that impact the way you treat not only yourself, but those around you. Gratitude is strengthened if you are intentional in the way you seek out and identify specific acts for which you can, and should, be grateful.

The American Psychological Association has determined that we perceive an act as more worthy of gratitude when:

1) It cost someone (either time or effort)

2) It is perceived to be of value

3) It is not obligatory or habitual in nature

4) The result produces relief or happiness

Most FBI agents and law enforcement officers enter their career with the hope of arresting criminals who exploit the needs and weaknesses of others. Over time, however, their idealism is threatened because life is rarely lived in absolutes.

The black and white of justice frequently morphs into shades of gray; good is often found in the midst of the bad, and bad sometimes results from good intentions. Mental toughness is learning how to live with the paradox of contradiction and not run from the mystery of life. It's especially important to keep focused on being grateful when life is taking a down turn:

- Seek out events and people that represent the things that embody your moral standards
- Express gratitude when you see them

- Let go of your need for the "right" way to be "your" way
- Clarify what you know to be the truth in your heart, get to know it better
- Remember that truth is its own best argument

It's impossible to give full attention to both ego and gratitude at the same time. When you are appreciating something or someone else, your ego must move out of the way.

Deepak Chopra makes these points about ego and gratitude:

- Ego can get stuck on being right or wrong
- Real gratitude isn't passing and temporary
- Gratitude takes openness and the willingness to set your ego aside
- No one is grateful for things they think they deserve.
- Gratitude is unearned, like grace

- When it is deeply felt, gratitude applies to everything, not simply to good things you hope will come your way

Gratitude is an emotion that can be strengthened over time. It will take mental toughness to 1) intentionally seek out and find the people and circumstances for which we can be grateful; 2) remain focused on the priority of being grateful, especially in tough times; and 3) demand the ego to be put it in its proper place.

# Chapter 2

# *How Women Leaders Can Kick Butt*

I knew at an early age that I wanted to do something unique with my life. Perhaps that was because I spent my childhood being very ordinary; I lived for the day when I could break loose and prove to the world I had a champion's heart.

I found the story of Jael in the ancient book of the Bible to be one of the most inspirational stories I read as a young girl in Wyoming. It encouraged me to believe that I was capable of accomplishing great deeds, even in the face of tremendous adversity.

The story is found in the Book of Judges. Back then, a soldier named Sisera led the Canaanite army and commanded over nine hundred iron chariots. He had oppressed the Israelites for twenty years.

Sisera was brutal, and his own mother speculated that he was late getting home from a battle because he and his fellow warriors were dividing the plunder by raping women and hauling off valuables.

The prophetess Deborah was able to persuade a soldier named Barak to gather an Israelite force of ten thousand to fight the Canaanites—and Sisera was soundly defeated. Exhausted, he fled on foot to a nearby settlement that was known to be an ally of the Canaanites where he thought he could find safety.

A woman in that settlement named Jael saw Sisera approaching and went outside to meet him. She offered him hospitality by covering him with a rug and giving him both water and milk to drink.

Convinced she was harmless and willing to do his bidding, he told her to guard the tent entrance and let no one enter. He then fell into a weary sleep. Jael saw this as her opportunity and as soon as he was asleep, she picked up a hammer and tent peg and softly moved to Sisera's side.

She raised the hammer in one hand and drove the tent peg through Sisera's temple with such force that it stuck in the ground! When the Israelite soldiers came looking for Barak, Jael showed them Sisera's body. The Bible says there was peace for the next forty years.

The story of Jael illustrates the quiet strength of a woman who was as much of a champion as any hero from the ancient world, who are so often depicted as men.

# TIP #6

## *Strong Women Can Prevail Not Despite Their Sex, but Through Their Sex*

Jael used her feminine qualities to seduce Sisera into thinking all was well. She brings him milk to drink, she covers him with a rug, and yet this warm figure reaches for a tent stake and executes her enemy.

Women can prevail not despite, but through, their sex.

Time and time again I found that, as an FBI agent, people "let their guard down" when around me as I interviewed them. Holding the tension between gentleness and hard conviction takes mental toughness, and this tension is a unique tool that women can use to their advantage.

When I walked into my new FBI office, I was viewed as a curiosity more than anything else. In the 1980's there weren't that many female FBI agents; everyone was polite but distant. I wore a suit and low-heeled shoes—despite what is shown in movies and TV shows, nothing looks more ridiculous than a woman tottering around on high heels trying to balance the weight of a gun on her hip.

I pretended not to notice when the guys grabbed their jackets and headed out the door for lunch without inviting me. I also pretended not to notice that I wasn't included in the informal squad debriefings about the direction the more important cases were headed. Our squad worked counterintelligence and espionage and only senior agents were considered experienced enough to be investigating the activities of an intelligence officer.

It soon became evident that I would never get the opportunity as long as I was assigned the cases no one else on the squad wanted. If I wanted to work against a foreign spy, I'd need to go out and find one myself.

I could have been bitter; instead, I let this situation show me how to be better.

We've all been in situations where it's hard to keep a positive attitude. I'll admit that there were times I wanted to quit the squad and ask to be reassigned.

I did not leave the squad. Instead, I made a choice to be proactive. I crafted an undercover proposal where I would be the undercover agent in a position to target foreign spies visiting companies with classified or proprietary information. FBI Headquarters loved it because it was a fresh and unique approach. They liked the idea of a woman, who appeared less threatening than a man, mixing with the crowd that included our foreign spy.

# TIP #7

*Strong Women Never Allow Themselves to Be Imprisoned by Their Own Mind*

Jael is only one example of many women throughout history who were "the best man for the job."

There are more women than ever acting and living in non-traditional ways, so this might be the right time to rethink some of our assumptions: what is traditional, and why is traditional necessarily a better way of life?

Just because it's the way it's always been done doesn't mean it's the way it should always be done.

Few of us wake up each day and announce to the world that we are going to be a hero. Instead, most of us meet life each day with little fanfare and few fantasies about doing anything other than what is expected of us.

It is only when we're confronted with obstacles that threaten to derail our life's journey that we summon the determination to break through the barrier in front of us. Strong women never allow themselves to be imprisoned in their own mind by their circumstances or appearance.

# TIP #8

*Strong Women Summon the Courage to Find Meaning in Their Own Stories and Experiences*

Jael assumes the traditionally male role of assassin; however, the prophetess Deborah still called her the "most blessed of women." She did not lose her femininity because of her actions. Indeed, her actions were so effective because she used her feminine wiles.

Living a life of purpose and meaning requires the courage to take a chance. I'm not talking about the physical courage of a soldier or superhero—I mean the extraordinary, heroic courage demanded of each of us every day. It's the resolve to meet life's scary circumstances head on with confidence and determination.

Jael is only one in a long line of women over the centuries who have kicked butt. Thanks to women like her, there are more opportunities for many more extraordinary stories to be told.

It is the responsibility and duty of every leader to uncover the significance of their own story and experiences.

# Chapter 3

## *How to Get What You Want*

FBI counterintelligence agents, such as I, recruit foreign spies to work for the U.S. government. It's not that we are selling anything; instead, we are using persuasion to make our point. Very often, we are successful.

You may never find yourself in a situation where you'll be confronted with a Russian spy trying to steal classified information, and chances are even slimmer that you'll be asked to recruit him to work for our side, but there will be times that you will absolutely need to make your point.

Persuasion is not just for spies, salespeople, and teenagers.

46

You may need to persuade your boss to take a closer look at your proposal or persuade employees to perform better. If you are a leader, persuasion becomes even more important.

Leadership is, essentially, the ability to persuade others to keep moving toward goals. Persuasion is an important component of leadership because it means changing someone's mind. If the mind isn't changed, the person hasn't been persuaded. The art of getting what you want is learning how to evoke and shape emotional responses in others.

As Professor Robert Cialdini points out, getting what you want is the ability to be persuasive, not manipulative. It is the ability to manage the emotions of others and respond to their arguments.

# TIP #9

*Listen to What Others Have to Say*

An essential element of mental toughness is the ability to accurately read the emotions of others and then adapt your behavior accordingly.

If I wanted to recruit a foreign spy to work for the FBI, I needed to listen to them so I could match my personality to theirs. By matching my personality, I mean assess whether they were introverts or extroverts, analytical or visionary, purpose-driven or security-driven, goal-oriented or people-oriented. To be successful, you may need to match your personality to your boss, employee, or client.

Listening is the part of communicating that often gets short shrift in favor of talking, but if you want to be emotionally intelligent about others in your sphere, you will need to keep your mouth shut and ears open. It is impossible to listen to what others have to say if you are the one who is constantly talking.

Consultant and author Jesse Lyn Stoner suggests that many of us equate listening with problem-solving without realizing it. According to Stoner, "We believe that when someone shares a problem, the best response is to help them find a solution."

*"Most people do not listen with the intent to understand; they listen with the intent to reply"* – Stephen R. Covey

A few years ago I completed the Spiritual Exercises of Saint Ignatius of Loyola, a set of Christian meditations, prayers and mental exercises, carried out over a period of 30 consecutive days. Each day we were divided into groups of 6 to share our thoughts, reflections, and spiritual journey. One of the requirements of the group was to adhere to the rules of "sacred listening."

Sacred listening is the discipline of sitting in silence while another person speaks. There are no interruptions, offerings of advice, comments, or follow up questions. This gave us the freedom to do nothing except listen to the words of the person who was speaking. With sacred listening came the ability to hear emotions and discern which words were freighted with more meaning— even when they were not overtly expressed.

The ability to listen to the words of other people, absorb their full meaning without allowing our own mental chatter to interfere, or attempt to offer solutions more suited to our needs than theirs, is the hallmark of an emotionally intelligent leader.

# TIP #*10* *Build Relationships*

Only by taking the time to develop relationships, can you fully understand people's needs, desires, and fears. Until this happens, it's very difficult to engage them in any meaningful way.

This is difficult because it means you need to take the focus away from yourself and concentrate on the person in front of you—and this is true whether you're knee-to-knee with a person or in front of a computer screen answering emails. It means being present with both sides of the conversation—not just your side.

One of the smartest ways to make your life easy is to think positively about others.

- When you look for the good in others, often they will surprise you and show it.

- When you bring out the good in someone, often you'll find that you've discovered a powerful ally and a true friend in tough times.
- When you search for the good in others, you often discover it in yourself.

People may think that, as an FBI agent, I learned to look only for the worst in others. Not so. I discovered that no matter the offense or background, people respond positively when they are treated with dignity. If I could offer that bit of humanity to someone who had hit bottom, I had found a way to give my gift to another.

# TIP #11 *Show Respect for Others*

In a culture that at times seems to be losing its ability to have respect for the opposing point of view, it's important to give others the respect that is due to them without trying to belittle them in the process.

When making our point with others, we have two options: we can either manipulate people into adopting our view, or we can use different measures of persuasion.

- Manipulation is a favorite of bullies like Adolph Hitler—and the tactics used by slick advertising.
- Persuasion, on the other hand, is the ability to charm and influence others using subtle methods without denigrating the other person.

The differentiator between manipulation and persuasion is intent. When we are being manipulated, we often react by letting down our defenses. Manipulation is only effective in the short term, however, because there is a lack of positive experiences by the person who is being manipulated.

By showing respect for others, we never cross that line between manipulation and persuasion. In spite of what we read in novels and watch on television, FBI agents never resort to manipulative techniques such as blackmail and coercion if they intend to build long term relationships. The reason is simple: it doesn't work if they hope to create a bond of trust and credibility.

Since most of us live and work with people, be a smart leader by showing them respect and creating an environment where they feel acknowledged and appreciated.

# TIP #12

## *Tact Requires That You Think Before You Open Your Mouth*

A person with tact knows what to say or do to avoid giving offense. Tact is essential when dealing with difficult or delicate situations. Do not ask embarrassing questions that put people on the defensive.

Marie Forleo gives great advice on how to win an argument or move away from a confrontational situation. Our natural instinct is to become defensive if our point of view is challenged, but Marie suggests we disarm the potential argument by saying two words: "You're right." This immediately neutralizes the situation by showing respect for the other person's point of view—even if it does not coincide with your own. Once the other individual is disarmed, you can follow up with something like, "I see how you feel (or think), but here is another way to look at the situation..."

Perhaps the biggest tip for developing tact is this: think before you say something. When you say "you're right," make sure you mean it. Too often these same words are thrown out as a way of giving up on an argument or discussion.

Try role-playing with a friend and ask for their input. Disarm a heated argument with those two words, "You're right." And mean it! Ask your friend if you are coming across the way you want.

# TIP #13 *Add Value to the Conversation*

My years in the FBI were a grueling course in learning good manners because people were not going to talk to me, let alone follow me, unless I could engage them in a way that was meaningful and productive.

Demonstrate warmth first when connecting with others, develop a bond and then be competent in the work you do together.

Writer and speaker Kare Anderson provides excellent advice when she advises people to "go slow to go fast in growing a stronger bond with others." According to Anderson, it is important to notice when you see interest grow in the other person when in conversation—this is the hook. Ask follow up questions at that point, directly related to what you just said. When we do, we accomplish two things:

- Increase their openness towards you because you've demonstrated you care.
- Identified the hook that matters most to them in the conversation.

Now you are able to speak to them in ways that that are meaningful and add value to the conversation. It's impossible to change people's minds unless you take the time to develop more than shallow, fleeting relationships with them. It comes down to this: in a world of mass media you must learn how to charm people if you want to persuade them to take your point of view seriously.

# SECTION TWO
## *How to Bulletproof Your Brain*

Experts disagree on the best way to make complex or strategic decisions. The only area of agreement between them is that we need to find ways to get our brains working together so we are able to access more information to make better decisions. This means utilizing both the logical, thinking brain and the emotional, intuitive parts of our brain.

We all know how difficult it can be to control our thoughts at one time or another. Self-help books can prod us in the right direction, but neuroscience—the study of the brain—provides insight into how we can actually change the way our brain processes the information that we use to make decisions in both life and work.

Until recently, the brain was believed to be fully formed by the time we reached our early twenties. However, neuroscience has shown us that the brain continues to form new neurons and neural connections throughout life.

The forming of the new connections between neurons in the brain is known as neuroplasticity. It is why our brain never stops growing. Not only does neuroplasticity allow neurons to compensate for injury and disease, it can adjust our response to new situations and changes in our environment.

This has huge implications for leaders. We can learn how to bullet proof our brain and make it stronger by *choosing* our response to the adversity we face in life and work rather than *reacting* to it. This means that we do not need to be held captive to our behaviors, memories, and habits. We have much more control than we once believed; in effect, we can re-wire our brain.

We overrate the importance of "inherent talent" while vastly underestimating our own potential capabilities.

*Why do underdogs win? Underdogs win because they know they can*–Vala Afshar

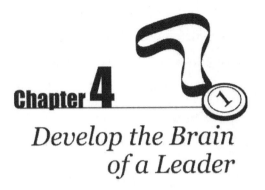

**Chapter 4**

# *Develop the Brain of a Leader*

FBI agents are required to qualify at firearms at least four times a year throughout their career. Years of training in mock arrest scenarios and target practice prepare agents to respond to threats automatically. When confronted with fast-moving situations, there is no time for decision making—they must rely on instinct to survive.

Training is an important component of mental toughness because training builds confidence, produces a sense of control, and provides insights into our behavior when we're pushed to our limits. These traits help successful leaders make good decisions in life.

Mental toughness is believing that while you may have only some control over your external circumstances, you have total control over your response to them. You understand the importance of preparing to win so you can be successful by knowing how to move ahead with a sense of fearlessness.

*"It's not the will to win that matters—everyone has that. It's the will to prepare to win that matters"*—Bear Bryant

As an FBI agent I dreaded Firearms Training. I shot over 3,000 rounds from my Smith & Wesson .38 caliber revolver before graduating from the FBI Academy. The soft flesh between my thumb and forefinger was bruised from the recoil. During the next 24 years I transitioned from a Sig Sauer automatic to a Glock, each gun requiring the same level of expertise and familiarity.

If confronted with the stress of a gunfight or arrest situation, it would be too late to stop and think about when and how to use my weapon. My training prepared me to make good decisions quickly.

Training so many times over the years etched a pattern of thinking into my subconscious mind that led to incredibly solid instincts. The power of repetition allowed me not only to anticipate my reactions, but also to review my performance in a timely manner. The lens of failure was the greatest teacher of all as I sought to master the unknown.

Each failure brought me closer to being successful.

Most successful leaders are instinctual decision-makers because they have made the decisions so many times in their career. They become immune to the pressure associated with decision making because they have learned the mastery of anticipating their patterns of behavior, finding opportunities in stressful situations, and overcoming obstacles. Here are similar steps you can take:

1) Prepare for your success by visualizing how you will succeed in various situations you might encounter in the future.

2) Use the power of repetition by rehearsing situations that might logically come up in a meeting or conversation with your boss.

3) Survive a stressful encounter by noticing how you responded in the past to similar encounters; evaluate your response by picking it apart to see where you could have reacted with greater strength or more compassion.

4) Practice your responses ahead of time so you can spend your energy evaluating what else is going on around you.

## HOW SUCCESSFUL LEADERS REALLY THINK

Before I entered the FBI Academy as a new agent, I had never shot a gun. My firearms instructor told me that all I needed to do was relax, breathe, and focus. The best shooters, he told me, are very present in the moment and not distracted by other thoughts.

He was right. Ironically, shooting at a target can be a Zen moment. If your mind is cluttered with thoughts and anxiety, you won't hit your mark. Good shooters let all of that go and become very mindful.

I had assumed that target practice would be a physical challenge; but much like golf, it takes as much mental discipline as physical ability to be successful. Shooting a gun shares many of the same characteristics as meditation. Both require the person to control their noisy inner world with a strength of mind that produces mental toughness.

Years later I learned in my meditation class that relaxed muscles send feedback to the brain that all is well in the world. It's no accident that meditation requires a place of seclusion where people feel safe.

Our inner desire to protect ourselves prevents us from taking risks when we face obstacles and adversity. As leaders, this can hold us back at crucial moments of decision making. Many times, our fear of vulnerability and avoidance of risk is rooted in an experience from the past that keeps rearing its ugly head.

Scientists have learned that activities like meditation can not only change our in several ways, but also it can change the way we think about our fear of vulnerability and risk.

The mental activity of meditation adds synaptic connections that thicken brain tissues over time in the regions handling control of attention and sensory awareness. It also increases serotonin, the neurotransmitter that helps regulate mood and sleep.

We can also change our brainwaves, because when we relax, we activate the left side of our frontal lobes, and it is the frontal lobes which produce more positive emotions.

Looking for and finding ways to feel safer can control our hardwired tendency to hang on to our fear of harm, even when that threat has passed. Now, neuroscience is showing us how to create new ways of thinking that can harness our brain to help us be bigger, better, and bolder.

We've all been in tough situations where it's hard to keep positive about our situation. We can change the way our brain thinks about itself so it is more positive, however. We can build the mental toughness to rewrite the negative script that may be currently running in our brain.

Turns out that we have to intentionally choose to be positive because we all have an innate bias toward negativity. We process bad news faster than good news because our limbic brain system is survival driven. This explains why we're driven to avoid losses far more than we're driven to pursue gains. The limbic brain system is instinctive and creates the "fight" or "flight" reactions that have kept humans safe for centuries. Since the caveman days, it taught us how to get lunch, not BE lunch. Instinctively, it tells you to flee or withdraw, so you obey and say, "I can't."

You pull back. That's perfectly normal, but not everything that scares us, or is new or different, is a threat to our survival.

Scientific research shows us we can re-wire our brain. Below are some tips to keep in your toolbox to help you re-wire your brain when you need mental toughness.

# TIP #14

*Find Five Positive Thoughts to Counter Each One Negative Thought*

The brain rarely responds to positive words and thoughts because they're not a threat to our survival. Our brain doesn't need to respond as rapidly as it does with negative thoughts and words. It's naturally wired to pay more attention to negative rather than positive information because negative alerts us to emergencies and threats.

To overcome this natural bias toward negativity, we have to repeatedly and consciously generate as many positive thoughts as we can.

Psychologist Barbara Fredrickson recently updated her original research that asserted only 3 positive thoughts were needed to counter each one negative thought. Because our bias toward negativity is so strong, Fredrickson and others indicate that we need to increase the positivity ratio to 5:1.

Research has confirmed that when it comes to considering positive emotions, more is better. Sometimes you have to look really hard. Our ability to seek out and experience positive emotions depends on the thoughts that we focus on and how we interpret the events in our life.

When you are confronted with a negative thought, ask yourself these questions:

- *How have I overcome negative thoughts like this in the past?* If you've done it before, you can do it again.
- *Has negative thinking about this situation become a pattern in my life?* If you experience the same negative thoughts repeating themselves, you need to get to the root of why they keep cropping up.
- *Why am I thinking this way?* Challenge your thoughts by specifically identifying what triggered the negative thought.

- *Am I being objective and realistic?* Remember, just because you think something doesn't mean it's true.

- *Where is the evidence for the way I'm thinking?* Make sure you are not focusing only on the negatives and ignoring other, more useful information.

- *Is this as bad as I'm making it out to be?* You could be exaggerating the worse that could happen.

- *Am I jumping to conclusions without looking at all the facts?* Take a moment to look at the situation from the viewpoint of another person. If it helps, ask a friend their opinion.

- *How likely is it that the worst will happen?* Put thoughts into perspective.

- *What can I say to myself that will help me summon positive thoughts?* Identify positive aspects of your situation. Our biggest temptation is to feel sorry for ourselves and stop believing there is anything positive to be found.

Generating positive thoughts helps us overcome setbacks. It doesn't even matter if your positive thoughts are irrational; they'll still enhance your sense of happiness, wellbeing, and life satisfaction. They expand our awareness and attention to what is going on around us. This is a critical skill for leaders who are looking for opportunities and ways to solve problems. When we are able to take in more information, we can connect to other events going on in our peripheral vision, thereby expanding our understanding of our situation.

# TIP #15

## Reflect On Each Positive Thought for 20 Seconds

Rick Hanson's book, "The_Buddha's_Brain" gives us a wonderful and vivid illustration to differentiate between positive and negative thoughts:

Negative thoughts are like velcro; they stick.

Positive thoughts are like teflon; they fall away easily.

For positive thoughts to make their impact, we need to take the time to let each and every one of them soak in for 20 seconds. Our built-in bias toward negativity intensifies stress and saps motivation to keep moving forward. It also makes it harder to recollect and find positive reactions, so we need to intentionally enhance the way our brain forms positive thoughts. Here are some suggestions to help you:

1) *Pay extra attention to the good things in the world and in yourself.* Notice when things go well, when people treat you kindly, when you succeed at something. Do not be ignorant about the good things that are going on around you just because you are so pre-occupied with feeling sorry for yourself.

2) *Focus on the sensations and feelings in your positive experiences since they are the pathway to emotional memory.* Fleeting thoughts and feelings leave lasting impressions on your brain. This means the way in which we interpret our experiences really matter.

3) *Deliberately create positive experiences for yourself.* Recall times when you were happy, savor those experiences by letting them soak into both your mind and body.

# TIP #16

*Use One Brain to Talk to the Other One*

Move out of the emotional limbic system that is holding onto your fears by verbally describing to yourself what you feel when you're with people who are supportive and trustworthy. Write a message to the emotional limbic system describing the same thing. By using both verbal and written methods, you are forging more pathways into the thinking and logical cerebral brain.

Positivity is important. By teaching ourselves to react positively to our circumstances, we can override the amygdala, the emotional part of our brain regulating anxiety.

With the right self-talk, we can shift the way we see our stressors and become more flexible in the face of change and uncertainty. Fearlessness is recognizing that even in the roughest circumstances, we are never helpless.

The rigorous training of Special Forces is crafted so it creates the same fear that would be experienced in capture, interrogation, and torture. The fear produced by these exercises causes the stress hormone cortisol to spike about as much as in a patient undergoing heart surgery—about 20 times the normal rate.

Yale_Psychiatrist_Andy_Morgan has studied Special Forces soldiers for over a decade. His research has shown that those who successfully finish the training were found to have elevated levels of another hormone, called neuropeptide Y, which is believed to be a natural relaxant.

Morgan states that the way in which we talk to ourselves about stress and threatening situations influences our neurobiological response to it. Once you begin to express fear to yourself, *Oh my God, this is awful*, you begin releasing more cortisol. When you say, *I know what to do here*, this turns into a positive response and produces more neuropeptide Y.

# Upgrade Your Brain

After twenty years as an investigative agent, I was asked to be the spokesperson for the FBI in Northern California. It sounded like fun—even a little glamorous since I would be interviewed by local and national news media. So why did I hesitate when offered the job?

I realized that I would be moving from being the senior agent on my squad, and knowing everything about my job, to a new situation where I knew absolutely nothing. None of my former skills as an investigator had prepared me to handle probing questions from reporters, represent the FBI in news conferences, or prepare for live television interviews where I needed to come across as witty, credible and polished.

I am the type of person who comes up with the best retorts about twenty minutes after the question is asked—I needed to learn how to think quicker on my feet.

I was a beginner, starting over with a manual and basic training. My pride balked at being referred to as a trainee—my secretary, assistants, and clerks knew more about handling the media than I did!

I had to learn the ropes from the bottom up. It was tempting to feel humiliated by my lack of experience; instead, I felt humbled by all I had yet to learn.

There was no resentment, only a slow understanding that we are all students of life. Like all leaders, I needed to understand why having a beginner's mind was important to my future success.

With experience and practice, we can predict our response to the unknown with greater accuracy. A beginner's mind is opening up to the possibilities of what might be. It is a non-grasping, patient, and confident understanding of what it means to live to our fullest potential. It is having the mental toughness to always be humble, and always strive to reach peak performance.

How you do anything is how you do everything.

# TIP #17 *Keep Ego in Check*

The ego is always asking "How will this make me look? How will I benefit?" Ego looks for ways to prove it is right and others are wrong.

Leaders know that they can make a positive difference—but not the only difference. If they slip over the edge and start believing otherwise, they're no longer keeping ego in check; instead, they are suffering from the dreaded disease of *importantitus.*

1) When we keep ego in check, there is room for the wisdom of others to get in. We are able to listen more deeply, learn with an open mind, and adapt new skill sets.

2) When we allow ourselves the luxury of trial and error, like a child learning to walk, we experience a feel-good neurological response that can be stronger than the ego.

3) When tackling new and difficult challenges, we experience a rush of adrenaline, a hormone that makes us feel confident and motivated.

The beginner's mind does not need to prove or disprove anything. It has the humility to hold "what I do know" with "what I don't know." Holding this kind of tension leads to wisdom and not just easy answers.

# TIP #18 *Summon Courage*

It takes courage to move out of your comfort zone and into your zone of discomfort, where you feel awkward, clumsy, and alone. This can be especially difficult for leaders who feel they need to continue to hone their core competencies, but our comfort zone is a tremendous enemy of peak performance.

When leaders get into a comfort zone, they strive to stay right there—where they have found success. But it is the average leader who stops at success, because success and peak performance are often two different things.

It takes a strong mind to choose to move out of our comfort zone in pursuit of goals. If our goals do not have meaning and value for us, failure is enough to deter us from continuing in that same direction. So we try something else—until we eventually become successful at something. In the meantime, we stop asking ourselves whether we are moving down a path that still has heart for us.

When this happens, we suddenly realize that our entire life has been spent reinforcing mediocre performance.

It takes courage and mental toughness to continually move in the direction of your biggest goals and ambitions and not stop at success.

# TIP #19 *Avoid Stagnation*

The more accomplished we are at something, the harder it is to learn. Once we become experts in our field, the need to learn is no longer either urgent or necessary. This, in turn, increases the likelihood that we will fuse our skill with our identity.

Walking into a discomfort zone and risking failure threatens to unravel our identity. Our reaction to learning something new is often fierce and visceral because it can strike at the core of who we believe ourselves to be.

Once we choose not to learn, however, we risk stagnation.

Eric Kandel, who shared the Nobel Prize for Physiology in 2000, discovered the phenomenon of synaptic plasticity. As we try something new, we have to work at it. The nerve cells involved in that learning process fire a neurotransmitter to get the process started. The more effort we exert, the larger the synapses enlarge and the connections strengthen.

The more we stress our brain, those neural pathways get stronger. That is why practice—the repeated firing of neurons—leads to improved performance.

We rarely embrace hard work that stresses our brain, but our brain actually gets stronger from it. James Loehr, an expert on peak performance, says, "Stress (in moderation) is not the enemy in our life; paradoxically, it's the key to growth."

# TIP #20 *Enlarge Your Core Competency*

Moving out of our core competency leaves us feeling vulnerable and weak as leaders. We've become inured to having the right answers and confidence in our choices.

A beginner's mind, on the other hand, is flexible and agile as it leaves behind old assumptions and gropes for new ways to move forward.

This is exactly the mindset we need when confronted with obstacles and adversity! We may not be able to rely upon our developed skills when facing a new barrier or challenge, but if we've continually and deliberately placed ourselves in situations that are beyond our core competency, we are more prepared to deal with them when we're confronted with the unknown in life and business.

# Chapter 6

# YES is the Most Dangerous Word in The World

The only four letter word I never heard in my twenty-four year career in the FBI was "quit." No matter how tough the training got, or hard a case was to solve, or the size of the obstacle in front of me, I never allowed this word to weasel its way into my thinking.

A great deal of what I learned during my four months as a new agent in the FBI Academy had to do with overcoming obstacles and breaking barriers. Each of us was pushed to the limit of endurance and performance to where we wanted to say "I can't."

If we weren't pushed into our discomfort zone, the instructors weren't doing their job.

# CREATE NEW BRAIN CONNECTIONS

It takes positive thinking and mental toughness to create the strong mind needed to overcome obstacles and break through barriers.

When you reinforce a way of thinking, either new connections are formed or old ones are strengthened. So, when you maintain a strong mind that thinks in positive and constructive ways, these connections become more durable and easier to activate.

This is a tremendous concept, because it shows us how we can change our behavior. When we use the word yes, we are training our brain to make positive patterns more automatic. Since our brain is listening to everything we think about ourselves, we might as well start using words that inspire and expand our vision of our life.

Mental toughness is positive thinking on steroids. When confronted with obstacles and adversity, mental toughness is saying "Yes, I can do it...And I can do it bigger, better, bolder, and more badass than you think I can."

# TIP #21 *Choose Your Words With Care*

The words you use are important. Words originate in the brain and they have a lot of power because they energize our thoughts. Words are thoughts spoken out loud. The words we say to ourselves can either inspire or destroy, depending on what our brain hears.

When you think you can't accomplish a goal and want to quit, your brain puts barriers around achieving the goal; often these are no more than self-limiting barriers because you've told yourself you can't do it.

Choose your words wisely and speak them slowly. This allows you to interrupt your brain's natural inclination to be negative.

Words can change your brain, according to researchers Andrew Newberg, M.D. and Mark Robert Waldman. They suggest that the repetition of positive words like love, peace, and compassion will turn on specific genes that lower your physical and emotional stress. Once you do, you will feel better, live longer, and build deeper and more trusting relationships with others—in life and business.

# TIP #22 *Stop Using the Word No*

Researchers have determined that when you *see* the word NO for less than a second, your brain releases dozen of stress-producing hormones and neurotransmitters. These are the chemicals that interrupt the normal functioning of the brain and impair our logic.

Now, if you *say* the word NO, even more stress chemicals are released into your brain—and not just your brain, but into the brain of the listener as well.

The word NO and other negative messages interfere with the decision making centers of the brain, often causing a person to act irrationally. Mental toughness is being able to interrupt this flow of chemicals into the brain.

Every time you say "I CAN'T" you create a negative feedback loop in your brain that keeps getting stronger and stronger. Just like when we meditate, synaptic connections thicken the brain tissues over time. Only worrying, running away, and saying "I CAN'T" creates stronger and stronger negative messages you are telling yourself.

When you hear certain negative words, higher cognitive functions of the brain shut down. Your limbic system goes into survival mode and reinforces the "flight" or "flee" reaction that is always foremost in the amygdala. It's like any muscle—train your mental muscle to look for the positive.

If we focus on using positive words or images, we activate oxytocin, a neurochemical that helps trigger feelings such as well-being, affinity, and security.

# TIP #23

*Success Is Not About Being Male or Female; It's About Winning or Losing*

One of the questions I am most frequently asked is, "What was it like to be a female FBI agent?" Frequently the only woman on my squad, I had to learn how to survive in an atmosphere heavily laden with bias and testosterone.

My answer to this question is always the same: "I didn't have time to waste on that kind of bulls*#t. I had a job to do and had no time to focus on the stereotypes or prejudices that surrounded me."

Since I grew up on a remote cattle ranch, I learned how to focus on the important aspects of my environment at an early age:

—Be on the watch for snakes, but know the difference between poisonous ones and those that merely slow you down.

—When running a horse through a pasture, watch for badger holes that are big enough to break a horse's leg, but prairie dog holes are generally harmless.

In other words, be savvy enough to tell the difference between those things that can cause you harm and those that are merely inconvenient. When it came to thriving in a male dominated work environment, it took mental toughness.

Our basic survival instinct should alert us to the fact that we need to learn where the minefields are before taking a step. Whether it's fair or not, office politics has a great deal to do with career trajectory, for both males and females.

# TIP #24 Learn the Politics

The first thing FBI undercover agents do when embarking upon an new operation is "learn the lay of the land." It's important to learn the protocol and politics of their environment.

In the same way, you need to learn the politics of your environment—no matter where you are. As you already know, surveillance is a tried-and-true investigative technique utilized by the FBI. Here are three suggestions on how you can make it work for you to learn the politics of your environment: 1) Take the time to observe how upwardly mobile people in your organization navigate office politics, 2) Eliminate actions and manner that do not resonate with you or your personality/values, and 3) Copy patterns of behavior that are productive and can move you forward.

I found that many of the other female agents in the office assumed I would "buddy up" with them for lunch and coffee breaks. I quickly found out that about the only thing we had in common was the fact we were all women.

# TIP #25 *Create a "Hit List"*

In truth, I knew my strongest alliances would come from "buddying up" with the other guys on my squad. These were the agents with whom I shared cases and could discuss strategies. I chose to cultivate the right relationships, not the convenient ones. So, I identified four male agents who had good cases and the ear of the Front Office (FBI-speak for C-suite).

These four male agents were on my "hit list." They were the ones I went to for advice, questions, and general information. I buried my pride and ran ideas past them for their input on a case, and once they realized I was competent, they gave me solid advice.

In return, I updated them regularly on the progress of the case. Once they felt a degree of ownership in the way I was running an investigation, I frequently found them arguing on my behalf with our Supervisor when my decisions were questioned. Little by little, I penetrated into the heart of the Gang of Four. They gave me my big break when they recommended a case investigating the activities of a KGB officer recently arrived in San Francisco be assigned to me.

# TIP #26 *Stop Expecting Special Treatment*

Another female was eventually assigned to our squad and I was assigned as her training agent. I was always careful, however, not to act as though she was my new best friend; I treated every agent with the same amount of attention and respect.

Several female agents in the office had formed a group described by the male agents as the "Solidarity Sisters." The Solidarity Sisters did nothing but create opportunities for the male agents to justify ostracizing women from the Old Boys Network.

I understood the female agents' need and desire to support one another in a male dominated work environment, but I always felt it more important to forge out the message that 1) we are FBI agents, and 2) male or female...in that priority.

Neither the Solidarity Sisterhood nor the Old Boys Network worked and needed to be replaced. Until you are the one calling the shots, you need to understand how the Boss thinks. Make it your mission to decipher the goals and needs of those to whom you answer.

Don't expect another woman to give you a break because you're female. I wouldn't.

I'm not a believer in gender affirmative action. The only action people need to take is to kick butt and eliminate the competition, whether it's male or female. No excuses. No whining. No blaming others.

I learned my lessons by working in a tough environment, but competence always triumphed when it was mixed with a fair dose of savvy.

# SECTION THREE
## *Find Your Inner Warrior*

Our personal stories are powerful and they have meaning. Often, it takes mental toughness to excavate the significance of our stories and experiences because not all of our stories are warm and fuzzy.

*Sometimes things must change so you can change.*

*Sometimes you must break a little so you can peek inside to see the power of your own life and story.*

*Sometimes mistakes must be made so wisdom can be earned.*

*Sometimes rejecting barriers and obstacles is to reject life itself.*

Negative experiences can create negative reactions, but if we find our inner warrior, we can regulate our emotions. Managing our emotions is crucial because it allows us to use our brain more efficiently.

Most of us live and work in pressure cooker environments. We need to find healthy ways to cope with stress. If we don't, we often find ourselves in a cycle of self-sabotaging behavior in an attempt to rescue ourselves from our own negative feelings and attitudes.

A strong mind can pinpoint and control negative emotions before they diminish our capacity to stay focused and interfere with our decision making process.

The previous section was about bullet proofing your brain so it is stronger, flexible, and more agile. This section is about utilizing a strong mind to find your inner warrior and eliminate self-limiting beliefs that sabotage your efforts to move forward with success. The tips in this section are meant to provide you with a few tools to help you on your journey.

# Chapter 7

## *How to Stay Cool Under Pressure*

I watched as the FBI agent knocked on a red door with peeling paint and rusty hinges. When there was no answer, two fellow agents dressed in SWAT gear used a battering ram to break the door down—now it was missing a lot of red paint!

I was among the backup team that would walk through the house with weapons drawn to make sure there were no suspects hiding, ready to shoot anything that moved.

My hands were sweating and my mouth was dry, because no matter how many times we practiced this during FBI firearms training, this was the real thing.

I was under pressure—if I failed to spot an armed suspect it could mean life and death. Lots of questions were running through my head: What if I got shot? Would my bullet-proof vest keep me safe? What if the suspect resisted arrest? Did I have what it took to shoot him?

Instinctively, my brain was trying to keep me safe so it quickly identified everything that could go wrong. I had no time to think about the positive aspects of my situation—I was backed up by other FBI agents, we all had extensive training, and we all wore bullet-proof vests.

The best way to keep cool under pressure is to nip negative emotions in the bud before they manifest themselves. This is difficult because very often they are not within our sphere of awareness when they show up and sabotage our efforts.

By the way, we did not find the suspect in the house but he was arrested a few blocks away by an FBI surveillance team—without incident.

# TIP #27 *Complacency Will Kill You*

FBI agents know that emotions like fear and anger are OK. It's complacency that will kill them. A little emotion keeps them on their toes. Agents understand that an emotion like fear is their early warning system in fast-moving situations. Their awareness of the fear doesn't mean they back away from the unknown because they don't know what they'll find; instead, they move forward with caution and strategy.

The limbic system in our brain determines how we feel about our world at any given moment and it drives our behavior unconsciously. In a dangerous world, those who were alert and reacted swiftly were the ones who survived.

It is unlikely you will run toward your fear—or the bear in the woods—so you run away. The key word is run, because fear is a survival mechanism and demands an immediate response.

Your response to flee is perfectly normal, and while you may not be able to run away physically, you can turn heels and run mentally and emotionally.

To counter this, be aware of the things that trigger the limbic brain system and try to reduce them *before* they kick in. As we discussed in an earlier chapter, greater self-awareness is essential; everyone is afraid of a bear in the woods, but only you know what causes you to lose your cool under pressure.

1) Acknowledge your emotions for what they are rather than let them lead you toward poor judgments and irrational behavior.

2) Learn how your brain recruits parts of your body to express emotion. Pay attention to what your "gut" is trying to tell you.

3) Understand what you're feeling when you're feeling it. Emotions are often a pacifying system to deal with stress, and as such, can be excellent indicators of a change in your environment. They

are biological early warning systems that need your attention.

4) Arousal of the survival-driven brain can help you attain your goals by putting your brain on high alert. In this heightened state, it is better able to help you focus your sights so you can zero in on behavior that will lead to success.

# TIP #28
## *Notice Emotions When They Arise*

When your emotions are high, there are often not enough resources for conscious processing. The limbic system takes over and draws upon deeply embedded programming to protect you. Remember, the emotional limbic part of your brain is your survival instinct.

Since your brain is doing what it can with limited resources, it's easier to let unwanted thoughts remain foremost in your thinking.

It takes work to think about the way you think. If you don't have the extra mental energy—or time—to pause and think about your response, you will simply react to your circumstances because it's easier.

Train yourself to notice emotions as they arise during a normal day. Don't wait until you are in the middle of a crisis to notice when and how your emotions rise to the surface. Paying attention to them during calm times can help you nip destructive ones in the bud when you're under pressure.

# TIP #29

## *Change the Way You Look at Risk*

Author Michael Michalko reveals that before Thomas Edison hired a research assistant, he would invite the candidate over for a bowl of soup. If the person seasoned the soup before tasting it, Edison would not hire the candidate. He did not want people who had hard-wired assumptions about everyday life. If they thought the soup was not properly seasoned, it indicated a mindset that Edison felt would negatively influence the way they looked at risk and uncertainty. Instead, he wanted people who consistently challenged assumptions and tried different things.

Most of us are challenged enough in everyday life, without actively looking for more of them! But that is exactly what Edison felt stimulated a creative mindset. He understood the real genius in thriving with the uncertainty of risk was continually testing assumptions and challenging the status quo.

Follow these recommendations:

1) List your assumptions about a subject.

2) Challenge the fundamental assumptions by writing down the opposite of each assumption.

3) Ask yourself how to accomplish the opposite assumption.

When an experiment failed, Edison would always ask what the failure revealed and he would enthusiastically write down what he learned. He thrived on learning from his aborted ideas and experiments. He relentlessly recorded every problem in his notebooks. Whenever he succeeded with an idea, he would review his notebooks to rethink assumptions he'd made in the past.

# TIP #30

## *Resist the Urge to Judge Your Emotions*

We tend to treat our feelings as either enemies or friends. That is a simplistic, and childish, approach. We cannot divide our emotions into two piles: good and bad. Instead, we need to let them run their course, and remind ourselves that the feeling was there to help us understand something about the way our mind works.

As a leader, learn how to be bold and lean into your discomfort zone. The biggest obstacle to observing the entire range of your emotions is the tendency to avoid the ones that produce the most discomfort. If you try to avoid certain emotions because they are uncomfortable, you are caught off guard when they do rear their ugly head. Avoidance is a short-term fix. You'll never be able to manage yourself effectively if you ignore how to deal with the unpleasant stuff.

Don't minimize an emotion because it's not comfortable. You are being arrogant if you think you can control it by using this tactic. Instead, be bold and learn about the emotion so it no longer controls your behavior.

If you ever hope to find your inner warrior, you will need to be brave enough to label your emotion for what it really is once you notice it. Acknowledging a negative emotion does not mean you have empowered it to influence your behavior.

Research has shown that it is imperative how we bring emotions to the surface.

Once you notice an emotion, use a few words to describe it. Again, don't judge it but do voice your feelings. To stay cool under pressure, use a few words to label what you're feeling. This activity enables another part of the brain to open that will reduce the emotional impact of your limbic system.

A word of caution: describe your emotion in a word or two, and it helps to reduce the emotion.

Open up a dialogue about the emotion, however, and you increase it.

# Chapter 8

## *Ways to Grow Stronger from Turmoil in Your Life*

Lisa is a neighbor who recently lost her job, Mark is a good friend who found out that he has inoperable brain cancer, and Monika has learned that, against all odds, she is pregnant with her first child at the vintage age of 48.

All of these people were thrown into shock and turmoil, in part because they all seemed to live charmed lives in which they were in total control—until they got news that changed their circumstances forever.

As I listened to each of their stories, I was reminded of an old parable where a little boy is so discouraged that he was planning to quit school. His grandfather boiled three pots of water: into the first pot he placed a carrot, into the second pot an egg, and into the third pot coffee beans.

When the little boy asked what this was meant to teach him, the grandfather replied, "Each of these objects faced the same adversity—boiling water—but each reacted differently."

When adversity strikes, how do you respond? Are you the carrot that looks strong but becomes soft and loses strength? Are you the egg that does not appear to change on the outside but grows hardened inside? Or are you the coffee beans that learn how to adapt? As a result, they change the hot water, the very thing that brings pain, into something that is desirable.

It is not the experiences that are important; it's how we interpret them. It is our choice whether or not we grow stronger from them.

# TIP #*31* *Speak to Yourself in Ways That Are Positive*

The key to growth is the way we talk to ourselves. Mental toughness in the face of crisis and trauma is not simply about coping; it is intentionally choosing to change the way your see yourself and the significance of your story and experiences. It is no longer being a victim or a survivor—you are a thriver, and this will give you the hope you need to move toward growth.

According to former Navy SEAL Mark Divine, positive self-talk is an essential component in SEAL training and discipline.

If we speak positively to ourselves, we can override fear, worry, and anxiety when faced with adversity or trauma. Emotions are processed by the amygdala, a small almond-shaped brain system. Brain imaging has shown that negative emotions interfere with the brain's ability to solve problems and other cognitive functions.

Since the brain responds so powerfully to negative emotions, we must intentionally choose positive thoughts to interrupt the brain's tendency toward negativity to open the door for creative thinking.

Positive self-talk is a powerful way we can choose the voice to which we listen. We can talk ourselves into victory or defeat by focusing on opportunities and strengths instead of telling ourselves that our situation is dire.

A self-limiting belief is nothing more than negative self-talk. Self-limiting beliefs are mental blocks, negative thoughts, and unproductive behavioral patterns that have been stored in our minds—often since childhood. These negative patterns that keep repeating themselves limit our ability and program our mind to discard possibilities of achieving goals and success.

# TIP #*32* *Acknowledge All Emotions You are Experiencing*

Ignoring negative feelings is not healthy, nor is wallowing in them. If life has handed you a tough hand, remember that the only thing you may still have control over is your attitude. If you feel powerless because of your circumstances, it's because that is what you are telling yourself.

Suppressing our emotions doesn't work. We have to work very hard to shut an emotion down once it is up and running, and in the process, we often get more agitated and tense.

Emotions are fast. It takes about 100 milliseconds for our brain to react emotionally and about 600 milliseconds for our thinking brain, our cortex, to register the same reaction. Your body language is already sending out messages for the world to read before your thinking, cerebral brain registers what is going on. People around you may receive a more accurate message of what you're experiencing than you acknowledge to yourself.

Your circumstances may not be what you planned, or expected, but you still own your thoughts. Make them powerful.

# TIP #33 *Challenge Yourself to Be Brutally Honest*

When the chips are down, honesty is your best salvation. As a faith-based leader, I have found turmoil and adversity are the tools God often uses to break the hardened veneer created by our ego.

In FBI interviews and interrogations, a lot of attention is paid to the language used by the subjects of our investigations. Subjects will provide answers meant to please or assuage the situation, and while they are saying the right things, it is their bodies that betray them—they are lying!

If we are afraid, embarrassed, or angry, these emotions will "leak" through to our body language. We can often train our faces to be composed and not leak our real emotions, but we cannot control our body, and subsequent behavior, in the same way.

If there is not consistency between the words you use and your emotions, it will become apparent to your team members that you're faking it. Rumors will have a harder time getting started if the leader is brutally forthright and honest in their communications.

Self-awareness, or mindfulness, is the practice of thinking about the way you think.

As Danielle LaPorte reminds us, *"Wisdom comes from embracing contrasting experiences: a winning streak and a dark night of the soul."*

Often, those contrasting experiences produce habits that do not move us forward and ways of thinking that are negative. They're hard to change if we aren't aware of them. Here are two things you can do to become more honest with yourself:

1) Take negative reactions and feelings as clues that you need to probe deeper into where the

# TIP #34 *Develop a Mental Toughness Mindset*

A recent study of incoming cadets at West Point pinpointed the characteristics needed to complete the rigorous training. It was not athletic prowess, intelligence, or experience that predicted success; rather, mental toughness was a better predictor of success than any other characteristic.

Mental toughness requires people to pursue goals with a passion, not back down from challenges, not allow failure to define who they are, and not quit.

Psychologist Peter Clough and Doug Strycharczyk, authors of Developing Mental Toughness: Improving Performance, Wellbeing and Positive Behavior in Others, have identified four pillars of mental toughness:

- Challenge: seeing challenge as an opportunity
- Confidence: having high levels of self-belief

- Commitment: being able to stick to tasks
- Control: believing you are in control of your destiny

Let's take a closer at the mental toughness mindset:

## 1. MENTAL TOUGHNESS IS POSITIVITY ON STEROIDS

Psychologist Martin Seligman is working with the U.S. Army in fascinating research on Post Trauma Stress Disorder (PTSD). We all deal with stress, trauma, and crises in different ways. When faced with a traumatic event, most people react with symptoms of depression and anxiety, but within a month or so are physically and psychologically back to where they were before the trauma. That is resilience.

The study found that some have a tougher time and may need counseling and medication to get through. There are a few individuals, however, who actually have post-traumatic growth. They, too, first experience depression and anxiety, but within a year they are actually better off than they were before the trauma or crisis.

They have mental toughness. They learned from their experience and were stronger than when they started. Mental toughness is responding to stress with positivity instead of negativity.

## 2. MENTAL TOUGHNESS IS LEADING WITH VISION, NOT GOALS

When working an FBI counterintelligence investigation, the game plan was to recruit foreign spies to work for the U.S. government. If recruitment was my overall game plan, then my job was to set short and long-term goals that would move my investigation in the right direction.

Often, goals needed to be changed as new information became available. So while my approach would shift from time to time, the game plan never did.

Goals are essential if progress is to be made in life, but it's tempting to let them take the place of the bigger picture. If they do, it's harder to pivot and move in a new direction when events take an unexpected turn.

Goals are a measure of where we will be and when we will make it there. We try to predict how quickly we can make progress, even though we have no idea what circumstances or situations will arise along the way.

To thrive, use goals to plan your progress but rely on your vision to actually make progress.

## 3. MENTAL TOUGHNESS REQUIRES DEEP, MEANINGFUL RELATIONSHIPS

People who experience post traumatic growth are able to do so only when they deepen their relationships with others. Their depth and appreciation for those relationships is extraordinary.

Soldier Fitness programs have identified these key areas as essential for resilience and post traumatic growth:

1) Re-connecting with families, relatives, friends, co-workers, and neighbors. Positive growth from trauma is nurtured by supportive relationships.

2) Volunteering, in whatever capacity, to ease the pain and suffering of the general population. The benefit we receive when helping others is as great as the feelings of wellbeing from those we help.

3) Asking for help from other people when everything seems insurmountable. This is the time to let go of individualistic attitude in favor of collective efforts.

4) Turning to one's faith as a source of solace and comfort. Numerous studies have discovered

that religious and spiritual activities can moderate depression and stress.

We are all stronger than we think we are. If we remember that, we can focus on what we can do to change our behavior when adversity or crises comes upon us. Consider the words of Warren Buffett in a **Wall Street Journal** article: *"The truth is, everything that has happened in my life... that I thought was a crushing event at the time, has turned out for the better."*

# Chapter 9

## *How to Move Forward When You Feel Overwhelmed*

As the spokesperson for the FBI in Northern California, I was in a constant race to meet reporters' deadlines. Each day started with a new crisis, whether it was a bombing, kidnapping, or arrest—the flow of information into my office was overwhelming.

I discovered that 60 seconds is long enough to give a radio interview chocked full of information, and that five minutes is sufficient to prepare for a live TV interview. But, by the time I had replied to 40 emails, another 120 had appeared in my inbox!

I was under constant pressure from national and local reporters to comment on pending cases, yet if I inadvertently provided details of a case sealed by the U.S. Attorney's office to the media it would be grounds for dismissal and possible prosecution.

Lunch was optional, as were bathroom breaks. One of my assistants came into my office one day and said, "I can actually feel the stress in this room." I like adrenaline rushes, but the job was wearing on both my mind and body.

Many people feel the pressure of responsibilities, getting tasks done, and the constant overwhelming volume of work that is placed on their desk.

Feeling overwhelmed can leave us feeling so paralyzed that we become less and less productive, not only risking our job but also our health as well. We need mental toughness to put mental disciplines into place so we can move forward when we're feeling too much pressure.

# TIP #35 *Make Prioritizing a Priority*

Your brain uses energy like every other part of your body: a typical person's brain uses approximately 10.8 calories every hour. Since your brain is drained of power as you use it, this explains why it's easy to get distracted when you're tired or hungry.

Your best thinking lasts for a limited time. It's good for a sprint but it cannot take you through the day at the same pace.

Knowing this, start your day differently: since prioritizing your day's tasks takes energy, make this your first priority. Otherwise, you will end up feeling overwhelmed when you cannot see a way to get through your day's work.

Most non-urgent tasks can wait until you have time to do them. These tasks might be good ones to delegate to others. Learn to say "no" to projects that are not among your priorities.

# TIP #36 *Use Your Mind's Eye*

Visuals are a great way to activate the mind. That's why storytelling, pictures, and metaphors work so well—they generate an image. According to journalist Annie Murphy Paul, the brain does not make much of a distinction between reading about an experience and encountering it in real life; in each case, the same neurological regions are stimulated.

Brain scans are revealing that when we read detailed descriptions, evocative metaphors, or emotional reactions, our brain is stimulated. This can impact the way we act in life.

Visuals are laden with information. They provide color, shape, size, context, etc. Since they take less energy than words, they are efficient ways for the brain to process information.

Use visuals to represent each priority so you can see how it will look as you approach your goal and again as you tick it off your list.

# TIP #37 *Move It Out of Your Head*

Grab a pen and paper and write down your prioritized projects for the day. This saves your brain from the need to recall and review each one. Save your energy for getting those tasks done!

There are other benefits to using a journal and writing down our thoughts. We are tempted to type our notes because it can be easier and faster than longhand. That efficiency, however, may actually interfere with our ability to process new information.

Psychologists have discovered that students learn better when they take notes in the classroom by hand than when they type on a keyboard. New research suggests writing in longhand enables the student to both reflect and absorb information so there is better understanding and more memory encoding. The very act of putting it down on paper forces a person to focus on what is important.

# TIP #*38* *Find Your Optimal Time*

The idea is to schedule the tasks that take the most energy for when your brain is fresh and alert. Not everyone is a morning person, so perhaps you're most alert after you've exercised or taken a nap.

Understand the rhythm of your own body so you are aware of your own mental energy needs and schedule your priorities around them.

Most people respond to issues as they arise; instead, divide your day into blocks so you can schedule projects that require an agile mind during those times when your mind is freshest. Block out other times for routine tasks.

# TIP #39 *Simplify Complex Ideas*

Most successful leaders have learned how to simplify complicated ideas into a few core elements. It's the best way to make complex decisions. The elevator pitch was created to encourage entrepreneurs to succinctly summarize their business idea to investors into no more than 3 simple sentences.

This is incredibly difficult to do, but when you reduce complex ideas into a few simple concepts, it's far easier to access those ideas in your mind.

Salient, succinct, and specific points take less energy for the brain to process and provide effective visuals for the mind.

By following these steps, you can use mental toughness to learn how to discipline your mind and prevent it from feeling overwhelmed.

## GIVE YOUR CAREER A BOOST

"So, Jeremiah, if you're worn out in this footrace with men, what makes you think you can race against horses? If you can't keep your wits during times of calm, what's going to happen when trouble breaks loose?"—Jeremiah 12:5, The Message

Developing the mental toughness for top performance is not a modern day issue. This verse from the ancient book of the Bible get to the heart of it: if you want to run in the big race of real winners, it's going to take more than the mediocre performance that passes for success on an average day.

America has become a nation of bored insomniacs who settle for mediocrity in many areas of their life, but as the Bible verse above reminds us, it's a malaise that's been around for centuries.

Mediocrity will not sustain us when the going gets tough. Average people move from one failure to another until they finally find success at something, and then they stop. They have no idea of whether they've reached top performance because they are in a footrace with others who think like they do.

Success is enough for the mediocre performer.

To run against horses, however, means not letting obstacles or barriers that are bigger than you trample your goals when times get tough. Running at top performance will give you the edge you will need to keep moving forward.

Writer Marc Chernoff explains that in many cases you stay stuck in your old routine because it is familiar to you. You are afraid of failure, change, and the unknown. If you surround yourself with self-limiting beliefs that put your dreams on hold and make your goals smaller, you will pass up great opportunities for growth.

The only difference between a rut and a coffin are the dimensions.

Staying in a rut is another term for "rust-out." Rust-out is more common in America than in other developed countries and it's actually even scarier than "burnout" because, while burnout can wear down your body, rust-out can wipe out your soul and spirit.

*"Rust-out is the slow death that follows when we stop making the choices that keep life alive. It's the feeling of numbness that comes from taking the safe way, never accepting new challenges, continually surrendering to the day-to-day routine. Rust-out means we are no longer growing, but at best, are simply maintaining. It implies that we have traded the sensation of life for the security of a paycheck ... Rust-out is the opposite of burnout. Burnout is overdoing ... rust-out is underbeing."*

—RICHARD LEIDER and STEVE BUCHHOLTZ,
The Rustout Syndrome

Mental Toughness is the ability to get out of your rut by making mistakes, learning from them, and moving forward in a better direction. It will be stressful at times, but it will also restore your soul and spirit.

# TIP #40

## *Fire Up the Courage and Look Obstacles in the Eye*

Getting in shape to meet life's difficulties takes considerable effort and practice; it takes courage to make a change, step into the unknown, or confront an obstacle that looks to be bigger and stronger than you. But going back to the Jeremiah analogy: Do you want to shuffle with the crowd, or run with the horses?

You work an 80-hour week, are in a rocky marriage, and have a dead end job—Wow, and you are worried that a change will wreck your life! Really?

Do not give up, stop pretending that average is OK, admit things are not perfect, and find the courage to make a change.

*"I wanted you to see what real courage is, instead of getting the idea that courage is a man with a gun in his hand. It's when you know*

*you're licked before you begin, but you begin anyway and see it through no matter what"*— Atticus Finch, To Kill A Mockingbird

# TIP #41 *Embracing Failure is the Best Way to Learn. Really.*

If peak performance requires you to look at success differently, it will also require you to look at failure differently. You cannot avoid risk without avoiding life.

Hundreds of interviews have been conducted to determine the commonality between our greatest leaders. The conclusion of this research is that every successful person has endured failure. They had to overcome at least one major obstacle before they could experience success.

No one wants to talk about failure because as we fail, we puncture big wounds in our ego. It is precisely for this reason that we see important things about ourselves we couldn't see before.

The key to top performance is separating failure from defeat. They are two different things. We can fail time and time again but this does not mean we are defeated. We recover from a failure and grow into a truer understanding of the calling of our heart. This shift in mindset does not see failure as the end, but only an opportunity to try it again—this time differently.

*"When it's time to die, let us not discover that we have never lived"*—Henry David Thoreau

Our brain is wired to feel more rewarded when we can predict the future. Therefore, when confronted with uncertainty, we automatically feel threatened. To counter this instinctive reaction, intentionally move into sports, activities, or hobbies that produce fear, anger, and frustration.

Forget about being perfect—go ahead and push yourself to the point of failure! These activities will train your limbic brain to become more comfortable with uncertainty. You will also be able to predict your responses with more accuracy—something else your limbic brain will like.

Many times we are not confident we can overcome obstacles or break through barriers because we are programmed to be risk adverse. When we hit roadblocks, our automatic response is not to react in positive ways that will help us to overcome the adversity. Training ourselves to anticipate our responses allows us to control them.

*"A bend in the road is not the end of the road... unless you fail to make the turn"*—Author Unknown

Retreating from the rigors demanded of excellence is understandable. It is unlikely that Jeremiah was quick to respond. He weighed the options and counted the cost. The way he lived his life became the answer—he ran with the horses.

# SECTION FOUR
*Predict Your Success*

If I had to summarize what I have found to be true about developing mental toughness, it is this:

*I am only as strong as my greatest strength.*
*I am always stronger than my greatest weakness.*
*If I discover the worst about me, that discovery will be a new strength.*

Leaders need to be brutally honest with themselves if they plan to create the strong mind required to be successful. If you'll lie to yourself, you'll lie to anyone.

Successful leaders are positive thinkers who uncover their potential capabilities, and then *reach*. This means they stretch themselves beyond their current ability and spend time in their discomfort zone. It means intentionally reaching beyond their grasp, and not only expecting failure, but anticipating what it has to teach them. It means that they are continually looking to explore situations where it's not just about winning or losing, it's about what they learned about reaching their goal.

This is what I learned about predicting my success as an FBI agent:

- To increase safety, move toward the unknown.
- To increase chances for success, move toward the challenge.

When you are uncertain, or facing the unknown, move forward. The closer we get to our barriers, our self-limiting beliefs, the more we can educate ourselves about it.

The steps to follow and actions to take will not reveal themselves to us until we have moved closer to the very thing that creates fear inside us.

To conquer frustration, you must remain intensely focused on the outcome, not the obstacles. This section looks at what you need to do to reach your goal. The tips are simple strategies intended to nudge you into your discomfort zone and out of the shallow zone that can sometimes be interpreted as success, when in reality it is simply where you stopped on your way to something that holds more meaning and value for you.

*"The only difference between a rut and a coffin are the dimensions"*—Anonymous

# Chapter 10

## *Move Toward Peak Performance*

The ranch I grew up on in the middle of Wyoming was isolated so it was impossible for my brother and me to attend public schools. Instead, we had a private tutor. The only person I had to compete against in my class was me, so it was a continual game of personal best.

I worked hard to beat my own record, and my teacher would respond by saying, "Look at you—you've worked hard to get a better score."

As I've gotten older, I realize that my teacher's response was incredibly unusual. Instead, most teachers, parents, and others in the educational system respond with, "Look at you—you are so smart."

Without realizing it, my teacher had a growth mindset which believes that people get better by challenging themselves. The opposite represents a fixed mindset and is represented by how our educational system distributes grades and how most corporations conduct performance appraisals: talent is something that happens to you, not something you make happen.

Whether you have a fixed mindset or a growth mindset influences how you approach peak performance. Peak performance is successfully using mental toughness to develop the power of the mind and to practice mental skills training in every aspect of life. Often, the key to success is not found in our ability or talent. Instead, it is found in whether or not we believe it is something that can be developed.

Stanford University Psychologist Carol Dweck has discovered that people who are born with a fixed mindset often think of themselves as "that's how I was born." They can be driven to be successful, perform well, and look good. They also tend to receive criticism of their capabilities as criticism of themselves. This usually discourages the people around them from giving any negative feedback, thereby further isolating the leader from experiences and thinking that could generate change.

Fixed mindset leaders rationalize that luck is a significant contributor to success—especially in others. As a result, they often do not reach their full potential or improve with time because "that's how I was born." A fixed mindset gives them no tools for overcoming obstacles or breaking through barriers. Failure simply indicates they lack competence or potential.

How many of us know of people who live with this sort of thinking? How many of us live with it ourselves?

Leaders with a growth mindset, however, believe that intelligence can be developed and that the brain is like a muscle that can be trained. This leads to the desire to improve by embracing challenges.

Author Andrew Solomon writes, "The worst moments in our lives make us who we are." He has it right because growth mindsets embrace the challenges they come across in life, knowing that they will come out stronger on the other side. Obstacles do not discourage the mentally tough who have a growth mindset because their self-image is not tied to success; failure is an opportunity to learn—so whatever happens is a win.

If you are a leader who recognizes that they have a fixed mindset, it is possible to change from one to the other.

Follow the tips offered in this book and you will have the mental toughness to do so.

## WHAT GRABS OUR ATTENTION RULES OUR LIFE

Author Kare Anderson believes that what captures our attention rules our life. We intentionally focus our attention on what is important in our life and those areas we want to grow.

Our consciousness can handle only so much information, so we have selective attention. One key part of the brain which focuses our attention is the Reticular Activating System (RAS). It filters out important information that needs more attention from the unimportant that can be ignored. Without the RAS filter, we would be over-stimulated and distracted by noises from the environment around us.

Focusing on the goal and focusing our attention on the activity to achieve the goal at the same time overstimulates the brain.

Attaining a goal is something that happens in the future, and it pulls our attention away from where it needs to be in order to focus in the present moment. This explains why so many golfers miss a putt at the end of the final round or why football players drop the ball inches from the finish line.

They choke because their attention switched from the present and moved into the future. As a result, they lose their focus. Whatever we choose to focus our attention on will make it past the mind's filtering system.

# TIP #42

## *"Chunk It" So You Can Achieve Your Goal*

Successful people establish their goals. They visualize themselves achieving those goals. And then they break those goals down into tiny, clear chunks. Chunking tasks that are related is an efficient way to use the brain because the brain loves to make connections.

If you spend too much time contemplating the huge distance between where you are now and the goal you want to achieve, there is a risk you'll never get started.

Too much information can be as intimidating as it is inspiring. Break down your bigger goal into smaller chunks that will gradually get you to where you want to be.

Chunking is breaking down larger goals into achievable steps. This will help you understand all the tasks involved in achieving a big goal as well as create a timeline to get them done. By breaking down a huge project into smaller chunks, you can also experience the sense of achievement and progress.

Here's how:

1) Chunking often works best when you work backwards from your goal. Think about the obstacles you need to overcome, barriers you need to break, customers you need to contact, or product you need to produce if you want to be successful.

2) Investigate further to see if each goal you've listed above can be broken down even further into mini-goals. Take a closer look at each goal and see what steps are needed to achieve that specific goal.

3) Create a visual map if you're a visual person so you can get a picture of a) where you are, b) where you want to end up, and c) what needs to be done to accomplish it.

4) Put your tasks in chronological order, working out what jobs needs to be done a) first, b) alongside others, and c) alone.

5) Identify those tasks that will require more effort or additional training in order for you to accomplish them. If possible, choose the time you can tackle them rather than waiting until they are foisted upon you when you are least prepared to deal with them.

6) Build a timeline of your tasks. Decide when you need to reach your goal if you have the luxury of setting your own deadline. If you do not have that luxury, write the deadline down and then identify how much time you will need to accomplish each step and mini-goal. If you're pressed for time, how much of the work can you assign to others? Think about getting professional assistance if you need.

Successful people understand that clarity gives us certainty. Small, clear goals keep our attention focused and yet are not enough to stress us out.

# TIP #43
## *Look for Feedback to Help Move You in the Right Direction*

In order for feedback to be most effective, it needs to be immediate. The smaller the gap between output and feedback, the more we will know how to perform better. The reason is that our attention does not need to wander because the information is at hand.

If real-time feedback is not possible, find a way to measure your progress. It's important that your feedback loop is timely. For yourself, and others, tighten the feedback loop as much as possible—try to make it a daily habit.

No matter who you are or what you do, you need three types of friends in your life to help give you important and valuable feedback:

- The first type is the one you can call when things are going well and you need someone with whom to share the good news, someone who will be genuinely happy for you.

- The second type is the one you can call when things are going miserably and you need a listening ear.
- The third type of friend is the one who holds you accountable. Life is hard, and you need people who will stop you from feeling sorry for yourself so you can reach down and pull yourself back up by the bootstraps.

None of us have a magic ball to predict our future. However, we can be prepared for what we can't predict.

# TIP #44

## Stretch Yourself to Achieve Peak Performance

Unless you know your limits, you will not be able to prepare either your mind or your body to move past them. To move toward peak performance, you need to stretch your current skill level—but not so hard that you want to give up.

You will need to stretch yourself if you want to perform to your greatest potential. Exactly how much you need to stretch each time is debatable, but experts generally agree that the challenge should be 4% greater than either your skill or your last effort.

Increased stress will lead to increased performance—up to a certain degree. When you move beyond the healthy levels of stress, both performance and health will decline.

In high doses, stress can kill us. Ironically, it is also fundamental to psychological and physical growth. 4% growth is seen by researchers as the magical tension between challenge and skill. Most of us move past 4% increase in performance without noticing, and it's beneficial because this tension keeps us locked in the present and gives us enough confidence that we can do it again.

Our success begins and ends with a strong mind. We can move toward peak performance once we find ways to use our mind to do it.

A recent study by the_National Institute of Health tracked 30,000 adults over eight years asked participants a simple question: "Do you believe that stress is harmful for your health?" The study also tracked death records for these people over the eight-year period. The ironic outcome: people who died from stress died not from stress itself, but from the belief that stress was bad for them. Those who didn't believe it was harmful experienced no negative effects on their health.

In yet another study by the National Institute of Health, it was discovered that people have a "built in mechanism for stress resilience." It turns out your personal connections to the people you love and the simple act of giving to others can actually be an antidote for the negative effects of stress.

Health psychologist Kelly McGonigal urges people to see stress as a positive. In a TED talk she said that stress may only be bad for you if you believe that to be the case. When you choose to look at stress as helpful, you are creating the biology of courage. And when you choose to connect with others while under stress, you can create resilience.

# TIP #45 *Visualize Your Success*

The very act of giving your brain a detailed portrait of your end goal ensures the release of dopamine, a powerful mental toughness tool to steer you toward success.

I've always been afraid of water. To confront those fears, I decided to learn to scuba dive—even before I learned to swim. One of the requirements of scuba diving certification was to descend under water ten feet, take off my mask and mouthpiece, and then put them back on again. I was afraid I would drown in those few moments underwater and without oxygen.

What if I lost my mask? How would I get back to the surface? After all, I couldn't even swim. My instructor was with me, and during practice he had helped me several times. But on the day of certification I would need to do it on my own.

My fear of water had not subsided as I hoped it would. I did not feel safe in the water, especially when I was ten feet under.

The night before the test, I spent hours visualizing how I would take off the mask and replace it without drawing a breath or dropping the mask. I walked myself through the exercise time and time again. I saw myself taking a deep breath and then letting go of my mouthpiece. I watched myself pull off the mask with my left hand and hold it tightly as my right hand came around and pulled it back over my face. I thought about how eyes would sting from salt water if I opened them so I would keep them closed tightly. I then observed how I would grab hold of my mouthpiece and bring life-giving oxygen back into my lungs.

I rehearsed the sequence dozens of times. And when it came time for my scuba dive certification, I performed the underwater portion exactly as I had envisioned it. Later that day, I dove 100 feet down a seawall!

Little did I know at the time that the benefits of visualizing my performance were based on solid science. Achieving my goal was about more than work and discipline—it was also about physiology.

By visualizing my performance repeatedly, my brain stored that information as a success.

And with each success, our brain releases a neurotransmitter called dopamine. This is the chemical that becomes active when we encounter situations that are linked to rewards from the past. Dopamine enables us to not only see rewards, but to move toward those rewards.

This simple concept has implications far beyond scuba diving certification.

**BUSINESS LEADERSHIP**: Mental toughness is the ability to envision the outcome of an event to trigger the production of dopamine. Sometimes asking yourself a simple question such as, "What do I want this meeting to look like?" and then visualizing your performance is enough to get that important shot of dopamine. Start with visualizing every objection and/or question that is likely to come up in the meeting, and your response to it.

**PERSONAL LEADERSHIP**: Visualizing can help you see your own ability to perform in difficult or stressful situations. It can help take you beyond your self-limiting beliefs about yourself and move you beyond your current circumstances. Visualizing encourages leaders to ask "What if?" or "What else?" These types of questions open doors of possibility and opportunity. It's an invitation to move past the status quo.

**TEAM LEADERSHIP**: If dopamine is associated with increased creativity, leaders can use this knowledge to help their teams find ways to be creative in finding strategies that help them perform at levels that produce more satisfaction. Research has determined that dopamine is produced in anticipation of reward, not as the result of the reward.

From Victor Frankl: *"There's one reason why I'm here today. What kept me alive in a situation where others had given up hope and died was the dream that someday I'd be here telling you how I survived the concentration camps. I've never been here before. I've never seen any of you before. I've never given this speech before. But in my dreams I've stood before you in this room and said these words a thousand times."*

# *How to Beat the Odds*

Peak performance has been coined as a concept known as "flow." Flow is a state of mind during which we become so involved in an activity that the world seems to fade away and nothing else matters. When in a state of flow, times flies by, focus becomes sharp, and we experience a loss of self-consciousness.

We experience the flow of peak performance when we achieve a personal or collective goal. We also feel this "runner's high" when we are following our heart's calling and are truly engaged in something that gives us meaning and purpose.

Peak performance is about being your best so you can be successful. The ultimate definition of success is to realize our fullest potential so we can accomplish what we desire to accomplish.

# TIP #46

*Redefine the Meaning
of Struggle*

Dealing with struggle is the same in every learning cycle: we begin by overloading our brain with information. If you're an athlete, you will engage in serious physical training. If you're in marketing, you may begin with fact gathering. If you're a CEO, you may begin with a concentrated problem analysis.

Dr. Herbert Benson has discovered that an important chemical change takes place in our brain during struggle. Tensions rise, and frustrations, too. Adrenaline, cortisol, and norepinephrine are pumped into our system.

How we handle negative feelings during this stage is critical. We're struggling to identify patterns and then repeating those patterns so our brain eventually no longer sees them as a series of steps to be taken but as a chunk of activity. This definition of chunking allows the brain to simplify activities so it takes a very small bit of information and then predicts the outcome.

Dr. Richard Lazarus and his collaborator, Dr. Susan Folkman, have developed a theory of psychological stress that explains how we cope when confronted with trauma. Research has discovered that people who thrive during a struggle are those who think differently when confronted with a crisis. They are able to reframe the trauma in such a way that they can extract meaning from it.

Although they are able to reinterpret their situation, it is not blind optimism or disingenuous positive thinking that creates the change. The suffering is real; the difference is that they use positivity as a mental framework for turning their suffering into achievement and self-improvement.

People with strong minds often experience post-traumatic growth. Post-traumatic growth does not mean you will be free of the memories or grief. If you try to put your life back together and pretend that nothing has happened, you'll remain fractured and vulnerable. But if you accept the breakage, you can cultivate growth within yourself, become more resilient, and open to new ways of living.

As an FBI agent, I approached my obstacles as unsolved mysteries to be investigated.

A mystery requires us to look at a situation from many different angles, or through a larger frame. A mystery calls for us to change sides, back and forth, so we can see it from every aspect. No one solves a mystery by deciding on one conclusion from the outset and then force-feeding the facts so they fit their image of a successful outcome.

If we reframe our adversity to look more like mysteries to be solved by careful analysis, then we can pick away at suppositions and judgments which may, or may not, be accurate. We remain open-minded about how to solve the problem and overcome the obstacle.

# TIP #47

## Relax and Remember There is a Light at the End of the Tunnel

Researchers have found that to move out of the struggle phase, it's important to move into a state of mind where you take your thoughts off the problem. Once you can find a way to relax in the midst of your struggle, the stress hormones in your brain start to decrease and the feel-good chemicals like dopamine start to kick in.

This is why humor is so important in high-stress jobs. It can defuse an intense situation by letting the brain relax.

Keep in mind, as we previously discussed—the learning cycle is complete when you keep moving the 4% stretch along the continuum until you reach peak performance.

# TIP #48

## *48 Generate Many Failures to Ensure One Success*

Consider Thomas Edison: he was granted 1,093 patents for inventions that ranged from light bulbs to a talking doll. Edison believed that quality came out of quantity. He set idea quotas for all of his workers. His own quota was one minor invention every 10 days and one major invention every 6 months.

It took over 50,000 experiments to invent the alkaline cell battery and over 9,000 to perfect the light bulb. For every brilliant idea he had, there was a dud. Edison embraced uncertainty and risk when he set quotas for himself and his workers.

The initial ideas were of poorer quality than subsequent ones, because the non-creative ones were the first to be purged. The longer he worked at something, the more sophisticated and complex the idea. In the same way, you and I can hone our thinking and become more flexible in our thinking if we approach obstacles and failures as petri dish experiments that need to be refined.

About halfway through the FBI Academy I learned that climbing a twenty-foot rope was a physical requirement for new agents. The problem was everyone else in my class could do it—except me.

People who are physically strong are born knowing how to bend their bodies to perform unnatural acts while others, like me, find anything more than hunching over a book an unnatural contortion.

Day after day, time and time again, I'd get about one third of the way up and just couldn't pull myself up any further. I was fatigued, and at some point, avoiding rope burn became as much of a goal as climbing because I needed to get down safely.

It was humiliating to know that I needed to prepare for failure on each climb as well as prepare for eventual success. But this was the thing: over time I realized that the same skills I needed to prepare for failure would also be needed if I succeeded because I still had to get back *down* the rope.

Trust me when I say that retreating day after day was harder than moving ahead. I needed to think long term as well as short term. On one occasion I thought I might make it to the top if I really pushed, but how would I get down—with dignity and without injury?

The difference between successful people and those who are not is not a matter of how often they fail. Instead, it is a matter of how many times they try. Successful people fail just as often, perhaps more so because they keep picking themselves up again and again. They keep trying new things until at last they find something that works. They push past the negative attitudes and depression that comes with failure.

Failure is only a temporary condition; giving up is what makes it permanent. Keep moving forward. Listen to these wise words:

*"I've missed more than 9000 shots in my career. I've lost almost 300 games. 26 times I've been trusted to take the game winning shot and missed. I've failed over and over and over again in my life. And that is why I succeed."* Michael Jordan.

The reality is that you cannot fail; you can only produce results. Psychologists recommend you respond to these results with questions such as "What have I learned?" What did I discover that I didn't start out to discover?" "What worked, or what didn't work?" Mistakes are portals for discovery. When you try something and produce a result that you did not intend, but find interesting, pursue it.

It is a paradox of life that we have to learn to fail in order to succeed.

# Chapter 12

## How to Better Juggle Life and Work

One of the male FBI agents on my squad was talking about household chores that needed to get done, and then he ended the conversation with, "I'll let the wife handle it." As a female FBI agent carrying the same amount of assignments as my male counterpart, I couldn't help but spit out, "We could all use a good wife!"

My retort was met with silence but I had made my point: professional women are just as busy as their male counterparts. For those of us who don't have domestic help, it quickly becomes a situation of trying to balance two jobs at once.

While many men have taken on equal responsibility for child-rearing and home-maintenance, studies have found that most women still face an uphill battle when it comes to juggling their priorities.

Whether women resist giving up control at home, or whether the tasks are foisted upon them, it is clear that women need to rewire their thinking so they are more efficient at juggling multiple mental tasks to enhance their performance.

# TIP #49 *Forget About Multi-Tasking*

While it is possible to engage in several activities at once, it's also clear that accuracy and performance drops off quickly—for both men and women. There have been lots of articles written about how women can multi-task better than men, but there is very little science to back up this assertion. In fact, psychologists have only been able to confirm that men are slower than women when switching quickly *between* tasks.

The reason multi-tasking is not efficient is because the brain works in a serial manner: one thing after another.

People can observe multiple activities, but they are not able to pay equal attention to all of them. Women are told they can multi-task to meet the busy challenges of both life and work, but they are getting sucked into a lie—one with serious consequences.

Whenever we multi-task, or embark on more than one task that requires attention, research has shown that accuracy goes down. Psychologist George Armitage Miller was one of the founders of cognitive psychology. He discovered that our brain is not equipped for multitasking that requires brainpower. Our short-term memories can only store between five and nine things at once.

When you're trying to accomplish more than one task at a time, each one of them requires a certain level of attention. Your brain cannot process two simultaneous, separate streams of information and encode them fully into short-term memory.

# TIP #50 *Practice Routine Activities*

There are times, however, when we all need to perform more than one task at a time. One way to juggle more than one ball is to practice specific, routine activities over and over again until they become embedded. Once that activity is embedded, start layering by adding more activities.

Driving to work is a perfect example: you do not need to "think" about the route you drive, the radio station to select, which exit to take, or directions to your office.

These activities are embedded into your thinking because your brain likes to identify patterns.

The more you use a pattern, the less attention you will need to complete the task. Embed repetitive tasks as much as possible to free up your brain so you can focus on other tasks that arise during a busy day.

# TIP #51
## *51 Prioritize Information So You Can Make Better Decisions*

We've all experienced a barrage of information coming at us all at once. As a result, we sometimes get paralyzed and feel that we can't move ahead with any decision! This is a normal reaction because your brain is experiencing an overload of information that is queuing up for attention.

Just like a computer can get constipated with too many jobs coming in at once, our brain reacts in much the same way.

When confronted with chaos or bottlenecks, prioritize the information. Once you introduce order into the way you make your decisions, you will free up the brain's energy so it has more space for other information.

# TIP #52

## Be Wise in How You Split Your Attention

If you feel pressured by several things at once, make a conscious decision as to whether you should split your focus, and then put a time limit on how long you will spend splitting your attention.

Afterward, go back to focusing on your first priority. If a thought should enter your mind about another matter, jot a quick note to remind you at a later date and resume focusing on your priority.

If you're speaking during a meeting and you observe that people are splitting their attention by texting or checking email, announce that the next point you are going to make is important so you get their full attention.

Once the meeting drifts to topics of no direct relevance to you, you can begin to think of how to deal with other pressing matters by making notes or checking your own email.

It is possible to juggle several things at once, but remember, the only way to do multiple mental tasks, if accuracy is important, is by doing them one at a time.

Mental toughness is about working hard and working smart. If you have additional tips you would like to share, please feel free to share them with me by emailing me at info@LaRaeQuy.com. I would be delighted to consider including them in an updated version of this book at a later date.

Also, visit my Facebook page @ Empower The Leader in You. You will find related articles and continued discussions on how women leaders can use mental toughness in both work and life.

Check out my website at www.LaRaeQuy.com for more information on my coaching programs.

# Index of Resources

## SECTION ONE: USE EMOTIONAL INTELLIGENCE

Kare Anderson, Forbes, *"Catnip for Closer Conversations"*
Meghan Biro, Forbes, *"Leadership is About Emotion"*
Robert Cialdini, Influence: The Psychology of Persuasion
Deepak Chopra, www.DeepakChopra.com, *"The Use and Misuse of Gratitude"*
Marie Forleo, www.MarieForleo.com, *"How To Win Any Argument, Fast"*
Daniel Goleman, Emotional Intelligence
Jonathan Haidt, University of Virginia, *"The Moral Emotions"*
Michael E. McCullough, et al, American Psychological Association, *"Is Gratitude A Moral Affect?"*
Jesse Lyn Stoner, www.SeapointCenter.com, *"How to Really Listen"*

## SECTION TWO: BULLET PROOF YOUR BRAIN

Vala Afshar and Brad Martin, The Pursuit of Social Business Excellence

Benedict Carey, Los Angeles Times, "*A Mind To Survive*"

Richard Davidson, Jon Kabat-Zinn, et al, Psychosomatic Medicine, "*Alterations in Brain and Immune Function Produced by Mindfulness Meditation*"

Barbara Fredrickson, Positivity: Groundbreaking Research Reveals How to Embrace the Hidden Strength of Positive Emotions, Overcome Negativity, and Thrive

Rick Hanson, The Buddha's Brain

Eric Kandel, In Search of Memory: The Emergence of a New Science of Mind

Glenn Llopis, Forbes, "*The Most Successful Leaders Do 15 Things Automatically, Every Day*"

Margie Meacham, ASTD, "*How Words Affect our Brains*"

Andrew Newberg and Mark Robert Waldman, Words Can Change Your Brain: 12 Conversation Strategies to Build Trust, Resolve Conflict, and Increase Intimacy

## SECTION THREE: FIND YOUR INNER WARRIOR

Robert Brooks and Samuel Goldstein, The Power of Resilience: Achieving Balance, Confidence, and Personal Strength in Your Life

Marc Chernoff, www.MarcandAngel.com, Practical Tips for Productive Living, "*5 Things You Should Know About Letting Go*"

Peter Clough and Doug Strycharczyk, Developing Mental Toughness: Improving Performance, Wellbeing and Positive Behaviour in Others

Mark Divine, The Way of the Seal: Think Like an Elite Warrior to Lead and Succeed

Tony Fitzpatrick, Washington University in St. Louis, "*Everyday Clairvoyance: How your brain makes near-future predictions*"

Ferris Jabr, Scientific American, "*Does Thinking Really Hard Burn More Calories?*"

Sue Johnson, Psychology Today, "*Suppressing/Expressing Emotions*"

Danielle LaPorte, The Fire Starter Sessions: A Soulful + Practical Guide to Creating Success on Your Own Terms,

Richard Leider and Steven Buchholtz, The Rustout Syndrome

Michael Michalko, Creativity Portal, "*The Creative Thinking Habits of Thomas Edison*"

Rick Nauert, PsychCentral, "*The Science of Mindfulness Meditation*"

Pam A. Mueller and Daniel M. Oppenheimer, Psychological Science, "*The Pen Is Mightier Than the Keyboard*"

Eugene Peterson, The Message (translation of the Bible), Jeremiah 12:5

Annie Murphy Paul, New York Times, "*Your Brain on Fiction*"

Martin Seligman, Harvard Business Review, "*Building Resilience*"

Sue Shellenbarger, Wall Street Journal, *"Before They Were Titans, Moguls and Newsmakers, These People Were...Rejected"*
U.S. Department of the Navy, *Comprehensive Soldier Fitness Program*

## SECTION FOUR: PREDICT YOUR OWN SUCCESS

Kare Anderson, Forbes, *"What Captures Your Attention Controls Your Life"*
Herbert Benson and William Proctor, The Breakout Principle: How to Activate the Natural Trigger That Maximizes Creativity, Athletic Performance, Productivity and Personal Well-Being
Robert Cialdini, Influence: The Psychology of Persuasion
Mihaly Csikszentmihaly, Flow
Carol Dweck, Mindset: The New Psychology of Success
Viktor Frankl, Man's Search for Meaning
Stephen Joseph, Huffington Post, *"What Doesn't Kill Us: Post-traumatic Growth"*
Richard Lazarus, Stress, Appraisal, and Coping
Abraham Maslow, Maslow's Hierarchy of Needs
Kelly McGonigal, *www.KellyMcGonigal.com*
Douglas Merrill, Forbes, *"Why Multi-Tasking Doesn't Work"*
George Armitage Miller, *"The Magical Number Seven, Plus or Minus Two"*
Harold Pashler, Encyclopedia of The Mind

B. F. Skinner, Science and Human Behavior
Andrew Solomon, Far From the Tree: Parents, Children and the Search for Identity
Gijsbert Stoet, et al, BMC Psychology, "*Are Women Better Than Men at Multi-Tasking?*"
Stephen Wolfram, A New Kind of Science
U.S. National Library of Medicine, National Institute of Health, "*Does the Perception That Stress Affects Health Matter?*"
U.S. National Library of Medicine, National Institute of Health, "*Giving To Others And the Association Between Stress And Mortality*"

# Further Reading

*Moving From Me To We*, Kare Anderson

*Full Steam Ahead! Unleash the Power of Vision in Your Work and Your Life*, Ken Blanchard and Jesse Stoner

*The Power of Resilience: Achieving Balance, Confidence, and Personal Strength in Your Life*, Dr. Robert Brooks and Sam Goldstein

*Influence: The Psychology of Persuasion*, Robert Cialdini

*The 7 Habits of Highly Effective People: Powerful Lessons in Personal Change*, Stephen Covey

*Flow*, Mihalyi Csikszentmihalyi

*The Way of the Seal: Think Like an Elite Warrior to Lead and Succeed*, Mark Divine

*Mindset: The New Psychology of Success*, Carol Dweck

*Positivity: Groundbreaking Research Reveals How to Embrace the Hidden Strength of Positive*

*Emotions, Overcome Negativity, and Thrive,* Barbara Frederickson

*Give and Take: Why Helping Others Drives Our Success*, Adam Grant

*The Desire Map: A Guide to Creating Goals with Soul*, Danielle LaPorte

*Mental Toughness Training for Sports: Achieving Athletic Excellence*, James Loehr

*Creative Tinkering*, Michael Michalko

*Words Can Change Your Brain: 12 Conversation Strategies to Build Trust, Resolve Conflict, and Increase Intimacy*, Andrew Newberg, M.D. and Mark Robert Waldman

*Origins: How the Nine Months Before Birth Shape the Rest of Our Lives*, Annie Murphy Paul

*Quiet Leadership*, David Rock

*Learned Optimism: How to Change Your Mind and Your Life*, Martin Seligman

*Your Survival Instinct Is Killing You: Retrain Your Brain to Conquer Fear and Build Resilience*, Mark Schoen Ph.D

# Acknowledgements

I would like to thank the community of writers, leaders, coaches, and friends who contributed their ideas to this book. I have been inspired by Alli Polin, Chery Gegelman, Karin Hurt, Terri Klass, Cynthia Bazin, Michelle Glover, Kaylene Mathews, Steve Gutzler, Lolly Daskal, Tom Schulte, John Thurlbeck, Carol Dougherty, and Barry Smith.

I especially want to thank my good friend, Kare Anderson, who has been a steadfast supporter since we first met.

Thanks also to Anne Doyle for her brilliant illustrations and creative genius, to Roger, my underpaid editor, and Gus, my chief happiness officer. Thanks to my family, who taught me the value of strong minds and soft hearts.

# NOTES

# NOTES

# NOTES

Made in the USA
San Bernardino, CA
06 July 2018